Working With People

A Video Arts Guide

Video Arts is the world's leading producer and distributor of training videos. There are now over 150 Video Arts titles in daily use by some 100,000 organisations worldwide, spread throughout 60 countries. Between them they have won over 200 awards in major international festivals.

Video Arts programmes combine the highest standards of production excellence with the maximum training impact. The quality of the research, writing, activity and production is exceptional, and the 'So You Think You Can Manage' series is designed to make available this expertise, entertainment and long-established success in handy book form.

Working With People

Video Arts

*Cartoons by Shaun Williams,
Alan Hurst and Prototype Design*

Mandarin

This book is based on the following Video Arts training videos:

Straight Talking
From 'No' to 'Yes'
Talking To The Team
How Am I Doing?
The Dreaded Appraisal
I'd Like A Word With You
Who's In Charge?
This Is Going To Hurt Me More Than It Hurts You

A Mandarin Paperback
WORKING WITH PEOPLE

First published in Great Britain 1994
by Mandarin Paperbacks
an imprint of Reed Consumer Books Ltd
Michelin House, 81 Fulham Road, London SW3 6RB
and Auckland, Melbourne, Singapore and Toronto

Copyright © Video Arts Ltd 1994
Illustrations © Video Arts Ltd

A CIP catalogue record for this title
is available from the British Library
ISBN 0 7493 1837 6

Printed and bound in Great Britain
by Cox & Wyman Ltd, Reading, Berkshire

Contents

1 How to be assertive

If you are going to work successfully with your colleagues, superiors or subordinates, your customers or your clients, there is one vital area you will need to master. We'll call it being **assertive**. This is a technique, which like all other techniques, can be learned – provided you know the rules. It means getting your point across in the manner most likely to be effective, and though it sounds easy enough, most people fall all too often into one or other of the two traps of being too **aggressive** or too **submissive**. Both are counterproductive, making working relationships difficult or impossible.

Should you try to be assertive all the time? Well, yes. Because the kind of assertiveness we are talking about is a balance; an approach to expressing yourself with clarity without giving offence and without giving the impression that you think your views are always bound to be correct, which they won't be, or invariably not worth listening to, which again they won't be. In part you can think of assertiveness as a normal everyday strength – the strength of someone who *always* says what they have to say with the right degree of impact. This means doing so neither in such a way that you overpower others and build resentment or opposition, nor so ineffectually that you are ignored or misunderstood. However, in a business context it is useful to think of assertiveness as connected with **rights**; if we list some of these which will be familiar to all managers, you will see how important it is to be able to make your point effectively without confusing it with invariably 'getting your own way'.

> The right to hold and express your opinions, views and ideas
>
> The right to have your opinions, views and ideas listened to
>
> The right to have needs and wants that may differ from those of other people
>
> The right to ask (but not demand) that others respond to your needs and wants
>
> The right to refuse a request without feeling guilty or selfish
>
> The right to have feelings and express them
>
> The right to sometimes make mistakes
>
> The right to chose to say nothing on a particular issue

The right to have others respect your rights

The right to be clear about what is expected of you

The right to know how your seniors judge your performance

The right to get on with your job in your own way once objectives and guidelines have been agreed

The right to expect work of a quality standard from your colleagues at all levels

The right to criticise the work of others when it falls below a quality standard

The right to be consulted about decisions that affect you

Perhaps you are the submissive type? We must all, at some time or another, have left a meeting frustrated that what we had to say just wasn't listened to properly or that we felt inhibited from expressing an opinion at all. Some of this is to do with a person's character, perhaps a shy or reticent disposition. In this case two problems stand out: the first is that others don't listen, the second that you find yourself unable to say what's on your mind anyway. Imagine someone with the first of these problems – we will call him Colin – and someone with the second – we'll call her Marjorie. Now Colin's problem is that he simply cannot command attention. He is the sort who does his best, but when he attempts to say something in meetings he finds that others in the room whisper to each other, pass notes, make or take telephone calls. Every meeting or exchange becomes an unequal struggle. Colin and his ilk will become more and more confused, hesitant and apologetic, eventually grinding to a halt without anyone noticing and obviously without making the slightest impact with what, after all, may be a valuable contribution or piece of information.

And Marjorie's problem? She's the sort who simply cannot voice her opinions or objections. After a brisk statement her boss glares round and asks 'Any questions?' The Marjories of this world will stare at their notepads, say nothing, or murmur 'Fine', not understanding a word.

Why do we sometimes behave in these submissive ways? One reason is that we want to be liked, but forfeiting respect is no sure guide to popularity. No, just about the only advantage is that it avoids confrontation. Whereas a list of disadvantages . . .

> Point of view ignored
> Rights neglected
> Resentment bottled up
> Lose confidence
> Contribution declines
> Demotivation
> Feel undervalued

. . . could go on for ever.

How should Colin and Marjorie cope? What can they do to stand up for themselves? The most likely thing they will do, with all that bottled up resentment, is to have the occasional uncharacteristic outburst, possibly even playing out some fantasy they have nursed during their periods of humiliation. In other words, they will have a rare bout of aggression, helping nobody and gaining a reputation for instability. Colin, for example, might well lose control at a meeting as he hears some all too familiar words:

> **Colleague:** Colin, did you say something? I'm sorry, we forgot you were here.
> **Colin:** I'm not. I'm not here. I left about an hour

ago. I'm now at home digging the garden.
Colleague: I don't quite follow.
Colin: Of course you don't follow, you don't listen, do you! Because I'm not important enough. But I'm going to become important to each and every one of you because I'm going to devote the rest of my life to persecuting each and every one of you in strange and unfathomable ways, beginning with nocturnal coffin deliveries . . .

At this point, if true to type, Colin will storm from the room, make for his office, feel better for about five minutes and then realise he has made a complete idiot of himself.

And Marjorie? She is the weak silent type. She works at a travel agent's whose manager has just introduced a new fare structure. It's complicated, and it will be her job to explain it. Normally, of course, her response to 'Any problems?' would be a resigned shake of the head. But she too can turn nasty:

Manager: Any problems with the new fares?
Marjorie: Just one. It's gobbledy-gook.
Manager: But I thought . . . I thought we all understood it.
Marjorie: Oh yes, *I* understand it. Of course I do, but what about the customers? I mean, someone comes in here and wants to know how much for a weekend in Paris and it takes five hours to understand the answer. Well, I don't happen to have five hours to spare every time someone comes in. It's absolutely ridiculous.

Some people, of course, behave in these kinds of aggressive ways naturally. Every company has its bullies, but if there are any advantages in such behaviour it can only be the temporary relief of the person who can think 'that was telling them', and get some pleasure from it. Of course no one will treat the aggressive type as a doormat, but they'll avoid him when they can. And the disadvantages are as glaring as those of leaning in the opposite direction:

> Gets people's backs up
> Others react defensively or aggressively
> Colleagues withhold information
> No one helps or co-operates

So, what's the answer? **Assertiveness** – a mid-way between two extremes, commanding respect but keeping co-operation. Returning to Colin's problem, he *could* have got the attention he needed as his colleagues whispered and passed notes. He could, for example, have addressed just one of them:

> **Colin:** John, I don't want to be rude, but it's clear that your mind – all of your minds – are on something else at the moment. I don't know how important that something is . . .
> **John:** Yes, sorry Colin. We were having a word about an internal problem.
> **Colin:** Well, put bluntly, what I have to say is crucial to all of us. I need ten minutes to explain our situation, and as long as you need to tell me yours. We can either talk about it now, or we can reschedule – I'd be equally happy with either.
> **John:** Point taken. Can you give me time to make one quick call?
> **Colin:** Of course.

Now Colin will get a hearing. He has been assertive without being aggressive. The focus of the meeting, when John has made his call, will be exactly where Colin needs it: on the information he wants to communicate and the feedback he needs. He has got attention by saying his piece with due and not undue emphasis and spoken to *someone* as opposed to the generality of the air. Is there a comparable middle way for Marjorie's problem? Provided you can assemble your objections, or suggestions, in reasonable order (with a couple of quickly scribbled notes if appropriate), you need *never* feel inhibited about expressing yourself in what we are describing as an assertive way:

Manager: Everyone happy?

Marjorie: Not really . . . I find it confusing.

Manager: I beg your pardon?

Marjorie: Could you explain it again?

Manager: Oh, dear, oh dear, oh dear, Marjorie, everyone else seems quite happy with it . . .

Marjorie: Well, perhaps. But I don't understand it and I need to.

Manager: You want me to run over the whole thing again?

Marjorie: Please.

Manager: Oh, for goodness' sake!

Another colleague: Actually . . . I wasn't absolutely clear.

Manager: I'm sorry?

Yet another colleague: I'd quite like to hear it again, if that's all right by you.

And another: I'm a bit confused about a couple of points.

Marjorie: Could you explain it again?

Manager: Well, all right.

So Marjorie asserted herself, and in fact demonstrated one of the secrets of assertiveness. This is to be honest. Without honesty – that's being honest with ourselves and with other people – none of us can ever achieve balanced transactions. So the first rule of assertiveness is – **Be honest**. It is an immutable law of the universe that, outside of police states, honesty is *never* as dangerous as you think it's going to be. But it still worries us. If by nature we are a bit submissive, we think honesty will lead to a confrontation and the ceiling falling in. If by nature we are a bit dominant we imagine honesty will lead to our losing control of the situation and the ceiling falling in. Well it doesn't. Honesty breeds honesty. So honest criticism will work provided it's done assertively.

Colin's boss wants his opinion at a presentation. Submissive Colin would have answered 'Great', looking at the floor. Aggressive Colin would have said a truculent 'Not much'. Is honesty the best policy?

> **Boss:** I thought that went really well.
> **Colin:** To be honest, I think some parts could be better.
> **Boss:** . . . what do you mean?
> **Colin:** It's a good pitch, but now that we've used it a few times I think I can see some places we could tighten it up a bit and give it more impact.
> **Boss:** It's got plenty of impact.
> **Colin:** I just wonder if we don't spend a bit too long blowing our own trumpet, and not enough on actually explaining what the machine does. I think that might give the presentation more impact.
> **Boss:** I like the impact.
> **Colin:** All I'm suggesting is shortening the opening by a few minutes. And maybe changing the music to something a bit livelier.

> **Boss:** . . . yes?
> **Colin:** The second video we show. I wonder if we could find something a bit . . . more to the point.
> **Boss:** What else?
> **Colin:** Well, I'd have to go through the script . . .
> **Boss:** I'm not sure I agree, but if you feel strongly about it, why don't you put something down on paper . . .

There we are, a rational discussion between two adults, not Armageddon. Colin may be right, he may be wrong – either way he asserted himself by being honest. After all, honesty makes communication possible because then people can actually find out what they all really think. Simple . . . or is it? Let's have a look at the versatile Marjorie, looking at a travel brochure with the designer, Simon. She is honest:

> **Simon:** So you don't like it.
> **Marjorie:** Well, it's very well done, Simon. But it's not what I asked for.
> **Simon:** I know, but I thought it might look more stylish if I gave it a sort of art deco look . . .
> **Marjorie:** All you graphics people ever think about is style, isn't it? Never *function* – never 'is it useful?' or 'does it do the job?' or 'can anybody read it?' Just style, style, style – you never seem to grow up, you still think you're in some comfortable, protected, self-indulgent womb of an eternal art school . . . you're like my little brother.

Yes, at least it was honest, but was it all **relevant**? Will it make it easier or harder for Marjorie to get her brochure redesigned? 'Honesty' needs to be qualified a little. Some emotions – and facts – are relevant; some are not. Deep down we're all emotional people, and we all carry around a lot of old emotional baggage – prejudices, class resentments, childhood dislikes, unrequited loves, Oedipus complexes, old stuff – we all have that. But when we're trying to get something done, we have to learn to differentiate between what's relevant and what's irrelevant, and stow the irrelevant baggage in the overhead compartment. And then we should be honest about the relevant facts and emotions – the ones which have a direct bearing on whatever we're discussing.

Let's highlight what's *irrelevant* in Marjorie's response and then add a more constructive approach.

> **Simon:** You don't like it.
>
> **Marjorie:** It's very well done, Simon, but it's not what I asked for.
>
> **Simon:** I know, but I thought it might look more stylish if I gave it a sort of art deco look . . .
>
> **Marjorie:** *All you graphics people ever think about is style, isn't it? . . . You never seem to grow up, you still think you're in some comfortable, protected, self-indulgent womb of an eternal art school . . . you're like my little brother.* Yes, I can see what you were trying to achieve, but the most important thing that the people who are going to read this brochure want is technical information . . . although it looks good, the artwork actually gets in the way of the spec. I mean, look at page 3 . . .

So, be honest about what's relevant – the most important lesson about assertiveness. Now we can move on and look at the situations where you may need to be assertive. Often there's going to be you and one or more other people and you'll all seem to want different things. The point of being assertive, honest and fair is that it helps the others to be the same, and that gives the best chance of reaching a satisfactory solution. Of course, there may not be one. There sometimes isn't. But if there is one, then being assertive gives you the best chance of finding it. But before you get into any kind of discussion you have to make up your mind what in the situation is negotiable and what is not – what's up for grabs and what isn't. And when you've figured out clearly what's **not negotiable** you must stick to it, you must stand your ground. Here's Colin again dealing with one of his colleagues who seems to have a big problem:

Ron: Colin, total emergency. I need the first quarter figures for a meeting this afternoon. Mrs Whiplash is after my blood . . .

Colin: This afternoon? I'm sorry Ron. I've just promised Sarah's complete audit by lunchtime. I just won't be able to do both.

Ron: Yes, but this is an emergency . . .

Colin: I'll have them for you as soon as I can, but I can't do them now.

Ron: Colin, look, if I don't give her those figures by two o'clock, I'm going to have to move to South America . . . Sarah won't mind . . .

Colin: But I promised.

Ron: Just ring her and tell her that the computer's crashed and you'll be a few hours late . . . *please*.

Colin: I can't.

Ron: Not can't – won't. You don't seem to understand, this really is an emergency.

Colin: It is for you.

Ron: Oh, don't be so bloody self-righteous about it.

Colin: Listen Ron. I don't want to get into an argument about this . . .

Which is exactly what he is about to do. There is a simple technique for avoiding this. If your position is absolutely not negotiable, just **repeat it**, firmly, politely, in such a way that whatever phrases you use you keep it impersonal. You are not rejecting a person if you refuse a request . . .

> **Ron:** Colin, total emergency. I need the first quarter figures for a meeting this afternoon. Mrs Whiplash is after my blood . . .
> **Colin:** I'm sorry, I just promised Sarah a complete audit by lunchtime, and I just can't give you the figures by two. I would if I could, but I simply can't.

> **Ron:** But this is an emergency . . .
> **Colin:** I'll let you have them as soon as I can, but I can't give them to you by two.
> **Ron:** But Colin, if I don't have those figures by two o'clock, I'm going to have to move to South America . . . Sarah won't mind . . .

Colin: Sorry Ron. I understand your problem, but I've already promised Sarah and I just can't do them by two.

Ron: Not can't – won't. You don't seem to understand that this really is an emergency.

Colin: I'll have them for you as soon as I can, but I can't give them to you by two.

Ron: Don't be so bloody self-righteous about it.

Colin: But I could probably manage something by mid-afternoon. Say about four o'clock.

Ron: I've got to have them by two o'clock.

Colin: I simply can't have them by then.

Ron: Four o'clock . . . Oh, all right. I'll see about getting the meeting delayed . . .

So that's the Instant Replay Technique. You think out what you're not prepared to negotiate about and then you just repeat calmly and firmly and nicely, again and again and again. In other words: stick to your bottom line. So now you – and the people you're dealing with – know what is not negotiable. Which means that everything else is. So, whether it's 'Who's going to make the coffee?' or 'Shall we buy General Motors?', you now have to go ahead and negotiate.

Finally, are there any assertive ways of responding to someone clearly not rational, in a mood, or a temper? Once again we'll drop in on Colin, faced with a very irate engineer and finding his assertive phrase-book going nowhere fast:

Engineer: You haven't got the faintest idea what you're talking about, pal. I've had it to here with you people, bunch of bleeding wimps the lot of you . . .

Colin: That's irrelevant.

Engineer: No it bloody well isn't . . . I don't have to do this job, you know . . .

Colin: I'm sorry that I spoke out of turn, but the bottom line is we have to get this machine back into production as quickly as possible. And I'm prepared to repeat that as often as necessary.

Engineer: . . . who says? Don't you get smart with me, pal . . .

How should Colin react? He can lose his temper. Or he can retreat. Or possibly he might even offer the engineer a cup of tea! Yes, **be sympathetic**. That's assertive. It's not submitting and it's not aggro. It's asserting sanity. And it's the final tip. If someone, for no apparent reason, behaves aggressively or emotionally towards you, try telling yourself that something unimaginably awful has just happened to them, and that you're the nearest upright object that they can find to take it out on. It may not be true, but if you behave as though it is, then there's at least a chance that you'll keep your own emotions under control, which always helps.

So that's assertiveness. To sum up as far as emotions and facts are concerned:

- Be honest about what's relevant
- Work out what's not negotiable, your bottom line
- Use the Instant Replay Technique to make sure you stick to it

When you do get to what is negotiable, try as far as possible to make sure both sides are in a rational frame of mind. In other words, start negotiating on equal terms.

The bad news is that assertiveness cannot guarantee that you get what you want. Nothing can do that. The good news is that assertiveness gives you the best chance of getting what you want. But even if it doesn't work out next time, at least (a) you know that you did explore all the options and (b) you will have laid the ground for a good working relationship in the future.

Golden rules

1 To be assertive is your right to be heard.
2 Aggressiveness and submissiveness get you nowhere.
3 Be honest and relevant.
4 Stick to facts, not personalities.
5 Know a bottom line and stick to it.

2 From no to yes – reaching agreement

We've looked at the advantages of the assertive approach.

Reaching agreement when various views
seem to be irreconcilable

Now let's look at handling people from a different angle
– **reaching agreement**, or at least the basis of agreement,
when various views seem to be irreconcilable. Can you
do this? Of course, some decisions don't need agreement,
they just happen, like the chosen dates for the Chairman's holidays. But on the whole nearly every decision,
from whether to cease trading because of insolvency to
whether to give a company party to say goodbye to a

departing colleague, needs some agreement by some group. Above all, within companies, specific departments and teams need to reach consensus either for action or to recommend action to the top bosses.

Quite a lot of us, alas, are like Martin, and we are going to follow his fortunes. He knows his own mind of course, but will his colleagues see sense? How can he bring those idiots to see that they're wrong? The problem has made him ill, and we find him in the doctor's surgery:

Doctor: Well, there's no real problem. Just this blood pressure. And the headaches and insomnia you talked about. Things all right at home?

Martin: Yes, fine.

Doctor: Work? Any problems with your department?

Martin: Not really . . . you know, the odd awkward customer.

Doctor: And your boss?

Martin: We get on fine.

Doctor: What about your colleagues?

Martin: My colleagues?

Doctor: They're difficult?

Martin: I wouldn't say difficult. They're just absolutely, totally impossible. I can cope with morons. I can cope with pigheaded people. I can cope with offensive people. But when it comes to knocking some sense into a bunch of pigheaded, offensive morons . . .

Doctor: Give me an example.

Martin: Ah, where do I start? Oh, I know, Tuesday. Department Heads' meeting. Simple problem. We all have different computers. It's getting more and more of a pain. The Board said they would replace them with a single, integrated system provided we could come up with a joint recommendation. All it wanted was a simple adult discussion, but do you think we could have one?

Now Martin's doctor is equipped not just with a shrewd mind but a rather special video which is designed to reduce waiting lists. He can use it to look at scenes past, present and future and switches it on to that fateful Tuesday. Three people, Martin, Brenda and Kevin, all use different computers and they have to reach agreement on just one uniform system. But can they?

Brenda: You see, we're getting very good results from the Textmaster now, and they say it could easily expand to service the whole unit. So it seems to me that that's the way we should go.

Martin: I disagree. Textmaster may be OK for word processing, but it can't handle the sort of storage and retrieval *we* need.

Brenda: But none of the other systems can edit text the way *we* need. Or if they can it takes ages.

Martin: Listen Brenda. It's the people out there we have to think of. The public, you know? Of course letters have to be written . . .

Brenda: It's not just letters . . .

Martin: Can I just finish my sentence? With your permission? If it's not too much trouble?

Kevin: Look, can't we forget about your two present systems?

Martin: Shut up, Kevin. Listen.

Brenda: Why don't you listen?

Martin: Because it's obvious. We can't propose a Textmaster system and that's that.

Brenda: Well, I'm not supporting anything else.

Martin: Oh, for heaven's sake, Brenda, don't be so childish.

Brenda: Childish? Me? When you're behaving like a spoilt schoolboy who won't play with anyone else's football?

Martin: OK. We stay as we are.

Brenda: But that's just stupid.

Martin: Right!

The doctor switches off, and Martin is confident of his support . . .

Martin: See what I mean?

Doctor: I do indeed. Quite ridiculous.

Martin: I mean, how do you deal with somebody so completely childish?

Doctor: She can't.

Martin: Exactly . . . what?

Doctor: What else did you expect her to do?

Martin: *Her*?

Doctor: Yes. Faced with your childish behaviour.

Martin: *Mine*?

Doctor: Of course. Look Martin, you've got children. And you know how when a child's got something to say it's incapable of listening? Well, that's your problem.

Martin: I do listen. I heard every word she said.

Doctor: You heard what she said. But you weren't listening. Listening is a skill. **Active listening**. You can't start to resolve a difference until the other person knows that their point is understood and taken seriously. You started with a classic howler. Absolute classic. It was the superb choice of the words 'I disagree'.

Martin: But I did disagree.

Doctor: Even so . . .

Martin: Oh, I see. Oh, I should have said, 'Yes, Brenda, I agree with your nit-witted, narrow-minded, pathetic, futile proposal, because I'm a moron too.'

Doctor: You don't have to agree.

Martin: Oh, wonderful. I don't have to agree and I mustn't disagree.

Doctor: Light is dawning.

Martin: What am I supposed to do?

Doctor: If you want to listen actively, the first thing you have to do is to **show them that you understand** that they have strong feelings. And pause to let them realise that you understand. And let off a bit more steam if they want to. That's the first rule. Now I'll write that out as a prescription and I want you to go back to where you started on Tuesday and take the medicine immediately. Then come and see me again and we'll examine the results.

So, if you reach an impasse, try active listening to find a way through. It beats a nervous breakdown and it's the constructive approach. Let's join Martin and his doctor as the video is switched on and they start to review the backwards-in-time results.

Brenda: You see, we're getting very good results from the Textmaster now and they say it could easily expand to service the whole unit. So it seems to me that's the way we should go.

Martin: I dis . . . sorry, that's interesting. Er . . . obviously you're very happy with Textmaster. It . . . does the things you want.

Brenda: Yes, it does.

Martin: What are the most important features? From

your point of view?
Brenda: Well, it's got very user-friendly software, and very fast editing.
Martin: Anything else?
Brenda: We've put in four months' training and we've put the data onto disc. People have just got used to it. They don't want to have to change again.
Martin: Well, I think the important thing is the people out there. The public. You know? The poor sods we're supposed to give a service to.

At this point the doctor, possibly worried about his own blood pressure, leaps up, switches off and glares at Martin:

Martin: What was wrong? I see. I should have said the public don't matter a damn so long as Brenda's letters are nicely typed. What does it matter if there's no one to send them to? We can always send memos to each other.
Doctor: You obviously feel strongly about that.
Martin: I do.
Doctor: And you seem to think that you have to jump in and contradict Brenda straightaway if you want her to listen to your point.
Martin: Well, of course I've got to . . . haven't I?
Doctor: In fact people listen to your point much better if they feel you've really listened to theirs. And taken it seriously. So hold your horses. Give her a chance to let off a bit more steam. And keep showing her you understand. There's really three stages in listening actively: show them you understand **that** they feel strongly, **what** they feel strongly about, and **why** they feel strongly about it.

Yes, Martin began well enough, showing an awareness that there could be legitimate views other than his own. But when it came to understanding the reason for Brenda's preference he was lamentable. So his medicine has to be strengthened, and the doctor sends him back to try again. We'll see what happens when they turn on the video for the next review:

> **Brenda:** We've put in four months' training and we've put the data on to disc. People have just got used to it. They don't want to change again.
> **Martin:** Well I think . . . You're concerned that switching to a new system could cause morale problems?
> **Brenda:** Exactly.
> **Martin:** Obviously that's an important point. So, whatever system we choose, you want user-friendly software, quick editing and something not too different for the users?
> **Brenda:** That's right. Oh, and it's got to take at least twelve VDUs, like Textmaster.
> **Martin:** But what's Textmaster like at storage and retrieval? And number-crunching?
> **Brenda:** Adequate.
> **Kevin:** Adequate for *our* purposes?
> **Brenda:** I don't know.
> **Martin:** Anyway, you definitely feel we should stick with Textmaster because you need the text handling. And because of the problems of learning a new system.
> **Brenda:** When we've only just mastered this one.

Back in the surgery, Martin and his doctor review what has been a much more successful encounter.

> **Doctor:** You see? Once she knew you were listening,

she behaved like an adult.

Martin: Yes, that's . . . very useful. Active listening . . .

Doctor: Which means?

Martin: It means . . . show them you understand:
> That they feel strongly
> What they feel strongly about
> Why they feel strongly about it.

Doctor: And pause for a response.

Martin: Good. I'll remember that. Thanks. Well, goodbye.

Doctor: Hold on. Active listening is only part of it. People who can't listen usually can't get listened to either. Do you have problems getting your ideas listened to?

Martin: No, that's not my problem. It's theirs. They never listen to a word I'm saying. It's like talking to a brick wall. Worse – at least a brick wall lets you finish your sentence. That computer meeting was an example. They were dreadful.

Doctor: Well, let's have a look then . . .

The video is once again called into action and Black Tuesday comes to the screen:

Brenda: Childish? Me? When you're behaving like a spoilt schoolboy who won't play with anyone else's football.

Martin: OK. We stay as we are.

Brenda: But that's just stupid.

Martin: Right!

Brenda: OK then. What's your idea?

Martin: Well, it's obvious. It's got to be a people-based system. People are the heart of the organisation.

Kevin: No, they're not. Figures are the first thing.

Martin: There wouldn't be any figures without people. For a start there's the supplier list, the user list, the contact list. There's a whole lot of . . .

Kevin: And what about accounts? What about budgets? What about invoices?

Martin: They're just secondary. Look, we've been enhancing and developing our Unitask system over three years. It's transformed our operation. It can handle accounts and word processing.

Kevin: Nothing like as fast as Datamax.

Brenda: And it can only take ten VDUs maximum. And the software's rotten.

Martin: Nothing's perfect. Obviously there have to be compromises.

Kevin: And you're going to have to make some of them.

Martin: Look Kevin. I'm not arguing with you. I'm telling you.

Once again the doctor is compelled for the sake of his own health to switch off with a strangled cry of 'Enough!'

Martin: What's wrong now?

Doctor: They won't listen? Like talking to a brick wall?

Martin: Look, if they'd been reasonable people . . .

Doctor: They *are* reasonable people. When they're presented with reasoned arguments. Contradicting them and laying down the law turns reasonable people into raving monsters.

Martin: But if they're wrong . . .

Doctor: But if you *think* they're wrong you have to make them realise it.

Martin: So you just have to contradict them.

Doctor: No. Just tell them how you *feel* about it, and why, then pause. They can't argue with how you feel. That's the first skill of winning yourself a hearing. Now go back to the office, back to that meeting, repeat the dose and see if you can begin to make just a little more progress?

And this is what comes up when it's time for the next viewing:

Brenda: . . . twelve VDUs, like Textmaster.
Martin: But what's Textmaster like at storage and retrieval? And number-crunching?
Brenda: Adequate.
Kevin: Adequate for our purposes?
Brenda: I don't know.
Martin: You see, Brenda, what worries me is whether Textmaster can cope with all the analytical work. We need capacity for sixty thousand names, at least.
Brenda: It can handle that number, off line.
Martin: Yes, but it's got to be on line for analysis.
Brenda: Well, I think it could cope. At a pinch.
Martin: But wouldn't it take up all the space for the other things you need, like text? And the user list is growing quite fast.

Martin's doctor gives a much more favourable diagnosis.

Doctor: Far better. You see you have got rid of the two destroyers of reasoned discussion which are contradictions and interruptions. And the three winners are always doubts, questions and information. You can't demand a responsive audience, you have to win yourself a hearing. And the first law of *that* is: **Explain your own feelings** in exactly the way you encouraged them to explain theirs. No flat assertions and contradictions. Just express your own misgivings, backed up by facts and not opinions. And pause to let them respond. Yes, I see signs of improvement, but we're not there yet.

Martin: We're not? What else did I do wrong? Everything I suppose.

Doctor: No, nothing, I mean it was something you didn't do. You never once took account of anything anyone else said.

Martin: I did. I heard it.

Doctor: But you never mentioned it. If you want people to listen to you, you have to prove you've been listening to them. That may mean paraphrasing what they've said. I see no real cure until you've learnt this absolutely fundamental lesson.

Once again Martin returns to his meeting. He has learned some of the ingredients of breaking through an apparent impasse: he has listened actively and responded with his own feelings. Can he now **involve** the others and go on to build some degree of consensus?

Martin: But then wouldn't it take up the space for all the other things you need, like text? And the user list is growing quite fast . . . You said you'd need at least twelve VDUs, didn't you?

Brenda: Yes.

Martin: Could the Textmaster handle twelve VDUs and 60,000 names? And Kevin's figures?

Brenda: It could be difficult.

Martin: I mean, I agree with you about your people having just mastered the Textmaster system. And Kevin, you said that you would need a greater capacity for accounts and invoices, didn't you?

Kevin: That's right.
Martin: It's a real problem. What do you think we should do?
Brenda: Is there another system that's similar to Textmaster? For the users, I mean.

Yes, the prescription is working:

Doctor: See how much it helps when you show them you are listening? So Rule Two:
> Explain your own feelings and refer back to their points.

And then do you remember the real killer? 'I'm not arguing with you, I'm telling you!' That sort of hectoring, domineering statement is a classic destroyer.
Martin: But you've got to say what you think.
Doctor: It's how you say it.
Martin: Oh, so you want me to be a shrinking violet?
Doctor: Absolutely not. That's just as bad as hectoring. But there is a way of making your point without being aggressive. What you have to do is to **make your point in a firm but friendly way**. Never show that your emotions are involved in a situation where you are seeking to discover and use input from colleagues.

Kevin: Look, I'm sorry to keep harping on about a Datamax but accounts and invoice payments are actually a legal requirement, and keeping financial records isn't just a luxury.
Martin: Of course not. I'm not saying . . .
Kevin: Nor is paying your bills. And Datamax has the best financial software.
Martin: Look, Kevin, I'm sorry but this really

matters to me. I'm not saying we shouldn't go the Datamax route. But what I am saying is that for our department's work, whatever system we choose, it has to be able to handle 60,000 names. Expandable to eighty.

Kevin: That's a hell of a big file!

Martin: I know. I wish we could do with less. But we can't. 60,000 is the minimum.

The atmosphere in the surgery, as indeed was the case in the office, becomes perceptibly friendlier.

Doctor: See? Everybody got your point and you didn't have to have a row. You didn't have to back down, and nor did they. Make your points firmly but stay friendly. So these are the techniques for getting people to listen to you:

> Explain your own feelings
> Refer back to their points
> Make your points firmly but stay friendly.

Martin: Hang on, how do you know all this?

Doctor: It's my job. I can't do anything for my patients unless I listen to them. And get them to listen to me.

Martin: But you don't have to do the hard bit, getting an agreed recommendation from the committee.

Doctor: I do really. Most prescriptions need the patients' consent, or they won't follow them.

Martin: Well, you're lucky Kevin and Brenda aren't your patients. They wouldn't even take an aspirin if they thought someone else had suggested it. Turn that thing on and see what happened after what you said was a howler . . .

The video button is pressed and the familiar meeting comes up again on screen:

Martin: Look, Kevin. I'm not arguing with you. I'm telling you.

Kevin: And I'm telling you. Unitask is a non-starter.

Martin: And your precious Datamax is a non-starter too.

Brenda: Look, isn't there some other system?

Martin: No, there isn't. We have a simple choice of one of our three systems.

Kevin: I don't see why.

Martin: I am telling you why. Because there are three systems. If we keep one, then only two people have to change. Got it? If we go for a fourth system, then everyone has to change.

Brenda: Then it has to be Textmaster.

Martin: It has to be Textmaster if getting everything typed clearly is what matters most. It has to be Datamax if doing accounts is what this organisation is here for. But if we're here to serve the public, you know, the people who pay our salaries, then it has to be Unitask. It's a very simple decision.

Brenda: I'm not supporting any recommendation for Unitask.

Kevin: Nor am I.

Martin: Fine. We'll let the Board decide.

Brenda: Let's toss for it.

Martin: No! You can't make decisions like that.

Kevin: We don't seem to be able to make them any other way. Heads or tails?

The doctor reaches rapidly for the control and turns to Martin.

Doctor: Well, it's always interesting to see sophisticated professional management in action.

Martin: I suppose *that* was my fault?

Doctor: You were fighting your corner.

Martin: Of course. That's my job.

Doctor: And you lost. But could there have been a joint solution?

Martin: Not as good.

Doctor: But presumably better than picking a system by the toss of a coin. In fact, there was a key moment when you could have got somewhere. Do you remember Brenda asking 'Isn't there some other system?' and you replied 'No, there isn't.'

Martin: But there wasn't! A fourth system was a non-starter.

Doctor: It might have been a bad idea. But it was a starter. You don't often get the whole solution at once. Brenda's contribution might have been the start of one, if you hadn't squashed it. And you'd started so well.

Martin: Had I?

Doctor: Yes. You'd demonstrated the first rule of working to a joint solution. You had asked for other people's ideas. **Asking for other people's ideas** is the first rule of working to a joint solution. And the second rule is: **build on their ideas**. Don't knock them down, the way you knocked down Brenda's.

Martin: But if they're not workable?

Doctor: Try to make them workable. Find something in the idea to build on. And a bit of encouragement gets more ideas flowing . . .

So Martin takes another trip in time and the result is viewed on the next visit to the surgery.

> **Brenda:** Look, isn't there some other system?
> **Martin:** No . . . some other system? That's an interesting thought. Do you know of one, Kevin?
> **Kevin:** Not really. Not to do what we want.
> **Martin:** Had you anything specific in mind?
> **Brenda:** No, but we don't know everything that's on the market.
> **Martin:** Yes, that's true. And for all we know, someone may be going to bring out a new model in the next six months.
> **Kevin:** That's possible.
> **Martin:** So we'll adjourn this meeting and do some investigation.
> **Kevin:** But we've got to recommend something before next year's budgets go in.
> **Brenda:** But I'm going on holiday.
> **Martin:** Oh, for heaven's sake!
> **Brenda:** I booked it six months ago. With three other people.
> **Martin:** All right. Then it will have to be Unitask.
> **Kevin:** Oh no it won't!
> **Brenda:** Not while I'm here.
> **Martin:** Then we'll wait till you're on holiday.

So near and yet so far! But there was a key moment where Martin could have stopped it getting out of hand again. The doctor explains:

> **Doctor:** It was all going so well, until you began laying down the law.
> **Martin:** I didn't.
> **Doctor:** 'So we'll adjourn the meeting and do some investigation.'

Martin: Well, obviously we had to.

Doctor: Even so, you mustn't impose your ideas. It doesn't work. Just *offer* them. And then you reverted to your own precious proposal without a thought for anyone else's problems. Remember that a joint solution will only come out of going some way to meet the needs of all concerned.

These are Martin's final prescriptions, to **offer his ideas** and to **seek joint agreement out of joint needs**. He attends his meeting for the last time:

Martin: And for all we know someone may be going to bring out a new model in the next six months.

Kevin: That's possible.

Martin: What should we do? Does it make sense to adjourn the meeting and do some investigation?

Kevin: There isn't time.

Brenda: Not with my holiday coming up.

Kevin: Suppose we tried to narrow it down a bit?

Martin: Well, let's see what we're looking for. A system that can handle lots of text quickly, and with an operating system not too different from your present one.

Brenda: With twelve VDUs.

Martin: Right. And with enough number-crunching for all Kevin's accounts and invoices.

Kevin: And you want the capacity to handle a sixty to eighty thousand name data base. I'm sure no one is working on a system like that.

Brenda: Better get one made then.

Kevin: Hey! Why don't we do that? I mean, if we got a consultant in and gave him that specification, he could find a way of combining the different systems to give us what we want.

Brenda: But wouldn't that cost a fortune?

Kevin: Not necessarily – anyway think of the cost of throwing out any of our systems and starting again.

Brenda: Do you think the Board would wear it?

Kevin: Yes, if we all recommend it, I'm sure they would.

Martin: Great. Well, I'm happy with that.

Brenda: So am I.

Kevin: Me too.

Martin: Well . . . we're all agreed then.

Golden rules

1 Always practise 'active listening'.
2 Show that you respect what others are saying.
3 Find out what others feel and let them know what you feel.
4 Don't confuse feelings with emotions.
5 Involve other parties to help find a solution.
6 Offer ideas, don't impose them.
7 A group looking for a solution must act like a group, not as individuals making up numbers.

3 Talking to your team

In almost all companies some kind of team meeting will be the most vital and regular form of communication. Board meetings, sales meetings, departmental meetings, ad hoc briefings, forward planning, 'brainstorming', reviewing results, target sessions, etc. etc., all involve teams of one sort or another. But holding them is one thing; holding them successfully is quite another.

We've all shared, or witnessed, Harry Willis's problem to some degree. His first attempt at a team meeting degenerated into farce and his experience will strike a chord in us all. Unlike Harry, however, we will not have had the good fortune to be monitored by someone like Mrs Hope, a true guardian angel figure of the business world, who is able to watch Harry's performance on her magic screen. We'll join her as she settles down in his office to watch him in action. Here he is, bright as a button, with a team consisting of himself, Arthur, Geoff, Sally, Rebecca and Bill. At least, that is the full complement but the last three have not turned up . . .

> **Harry:** Right, good morning everyone. Everybody . . . Well never mind. Right now I'd like to start by making what I think is a very important point. We really should be thinking, all of us . . .

But just then the phone on the wall behind Harry rings. Arthur picks it up.

Harry: Arthur, we are trying to hold a meeting here, so do you mind?
Arthur: It's for you.

Fatally, Harry takes his call.

Harry: Yes, now you promised you'd have my car ready by Thursday. A new fan belt, yes, well I think you'd probably better order one then. Right, 'bye . . . Sorry about that everyone. OK. Now this point . . . I think it is very important, in fact I think it's vital.

Another interruption. It's Bill, looking cross.

Bill: What's all this?
Harry: Team meeting, Bill.
Bill: Meeting? Nobody told me anything about a meeting.
Harry: Nobody told . . . Wait a minute, where's Sally?
Geoff: She's not here. Rebecca's not here either.
Harry: Well, why not? Surely they knew they were supposed to be here? I put up a notice on the board, you all should have read it. You know. I'm sorry . . . but I make no apology. Now . . .

With excellent timing the tea-lady puts in an appearance . . .

Harry: Could we wait for the tea, please? Er . . . we really should get on . . .
Arthur: Are there any biscuits?
Harry: We've got to get on.
Bill: Nobody's stopping you.
Arthur: I always have the cake with the cherry on top.

44

ER...

A good moment for the phone to ring again. Harry picks it up.

Harry: Yes? Six weeks to get a fan belt? How can it take six weeks? Mr Dixon, nowhere in this galaxy is six weeks away from your garage. Birmingham. I see. Well, goodbye to you . . . Right. Now then. As I was saying. 'Struth, what's that noise?

There is banging from the corridor. Harry goes out and finds a bloke in dungarees hammering a piece of wood.

Harry: Do you have to do that now? We've got a meeting.
Bloke: I've got to get it finished, haven't I? Don't know about no meetings.

Harry returns, defeated. Sally, meanwhile, has put in an appearance.

> **Harry:** Sorry about that everyone . . . right now, this first point as I say, is very important, in fact I think it's vital.
> **Sally:** Aren't we going to wait for Rebecca?
> **Harry:** Er . . . no we're not. One of you will have to fill her in later.
> **Sally:** Which one?
> **Harry:** Which one what?
> **Sally:** Which one of us will have to fill her in?
> **Harry:** Well, I don't know.

The phone rings again.

> **Harry:** Look, Dixon, I haven't asked you to build a time machine. I just want you to service my car . . .

And again, for Mrs Hope has seen quite enough for the time being.

> **Mrs Hope:** Mr Willis, it's Mrs Hope here. Might I suggest that you don't answer the phone while this meeting is in progress? And I'll be waiting in your office when you've finished, which I suggest you do right now . . .

Harry sprints out of the meeting to find her waiting for him as he dashes in, in rather worse shape than Napoleon during the Retreat from Moscow.

> **Harry:** Who on earth are you? How did you get in here?
> **Mrs Hope:** I'm Mrs Hope and I let myself in thank you very much. Now Mr Willis, about your meeting, how did it go?

Harry: . . . Go? It didn't go. I just don't understand why it all has to be such a performance.

Mrs Hope: But Mr Willis, that is precisely what it is.

Harry: What is what it is?

Mrs Hope: A meeting, any meeting, is a performance. And you, as team leader, are the producer.

Harry: Am I?

Mrs Hope: Of course. And there are some very simple rules to help you through your performance. First, you must **set the stage**.

Harry: What stage?

Mrs Hope: The stage where the performance is to take place. Now, to do that you must give the members of your team plenty of **advance notice** of when and where the meeting is to be held.

Harry: I did that! I put up a notice on the board this morning.

Mrs Hope: That's not enough. First of all, they have to know a couple of days before.

Harry: Yes, all right, that makes sense I suppose.

Mrs Hope: Now then, did you make any arrangements about the seating?

Harry: Well, I sat on a chair, if that's what you mean.

Mrs Hope: I meant for the members of your team.

Harry: Oh them, no. I think they prefer to stand really.

Mrs Hope: It's a performance, Mr Willis. You must **organise seating** so that everyone can see and therefore concentrate on what's happening.

Harry: . . . yes, I suppose so.

Mrs Hope: And thirdly, **avoid interruptions**.

Harry: Oh, come on. You can't avoid things like . . .

Mrs Hope: Of course you can't avoid every

interruption. But you can at least give yourself a chance, if you take the trouble to divert phone calls, coffee breaks, building works and all the rest of it.

Harry: Yes. I suppose I could at least do that.

Mrs Hope: Good. Because by doing that, Mr Willis, you will have set the stage.

Harry: . . . Yes, I like that, set the stage. Right. So, to set the stage I have first to give advance notice . . . organise seating so that everyone can concentrate on what's happening . . . and I have to, as far as possible, avoid interruptions. Yes. Simple really. I think I can get the hang of that. Setting the stage. It's not difficult really, bit of thought, bit of preparation, common sense really, what's the problem?

A rather smug Harry goes off confidently to the next team meeting. It is the same cast, but with unusual versatility they have become members of a hospital staff . . .

Harry: Right. Well, if you wouldn't mind all just bringing your chairs up to the table so we can all see what's going on. I've arranged for all calls to be held for the next twenty minutes. Has everyone got all the teas and coffees they want? Bill, let Geoff squeeze in there, will you? Now, Arthur, did you get them to lay off the building work in the corridor? Good. Excellent. Everybody here. Bill, Rebecca, good to have you with us.

Bill: Yes, sorry about the last one . . .

Rebecca: We didn't know when it was supposed to be . . .

Harry: Please, don't say another word about it. Erase it from your minds. It was entirely my fault. I didn't set the stage, you see.

Bill: You what?

Harry: Nothing. Now, there are a number of things I'd like to talk to you about this morning. Let's see . . . where shall we start? Er . . . be with you in a minute.

EXCUSE ME
A MOMENT . . .

Harry starts rummaging through a pile of papers. It is not a good idea.

Sally: What about the hospital postal service?

Harry: Ah, yes. I have got something about that . . . hold on a second . . .

Bill: Are we going to discuss the car park?

Harry: The car park? What about the car park?

Bill: Well, there's talk that we're going to be charged to use the car park.

Harry: Well now Bill, you see this is precisely why we have these team meetings. To put all of you exactly in the picture and cut short any idle speculation of that kind.

Bill: So are they or are they not going to charge us to use the car park?

Harry: . . . maybe.

Geoff: What's the news on the waste disposal routines?

Harry: Oh yes, good point Geoff. Yes, there is some news about that. And I'll tell you what it is as soon as I've found it . . .

Rebecca: As Marjorie's going on maternity leave next month, will someone be standing in for her?

Harry: Yes, I was going to mention that. That is a categorical 'yes'. Marjorie begins her maternity leave on the 10th, and her stand-in starts on the . . . well the 11th I should think. Now, the next point I wanted to make is . . . er . . .

The rummaging goes on and on . . .

Bill: Car park?

Geoff: About the waste disposal routines?

Sally: Hospital post?

Harry: Ah, here it is, and this may come as a bit of a surprise. It says that Marjorie is going to have a baby. So that's the news, and er . . . well done Marjorie.

Not surprisingly, the team are less than impressed, but Harry continues . . .

Harry: Now this is very important. Hospital activity is to go up by five per cent.

Bill: What does that mean?

Harry: It means, Bill, that the activity of the hospital is to go up – not down – up, by five per cent.

Bill: Yes, but how is that going to affect us?

Harry: Well . . . you work here, don't you? Pretty obvious I would have thought. Now, at the last meeting, some of you expressed some interest in opting out of our pension scheme, and applying to a personal one instead. I've had the forms distributed to you.

Rebecca: What do we do with the form when we've filled it in?

Harry: What do you do with it? You send it . . . or take it round by hand.

Rebecca: Where?

Harry: Yes I should think so. Ah now then, hold on, who wanted to know about the postal service?

Sally: Me.

Harry: Sally, right. I've got a note here. 'Hospital post'. Oh . . . hold on. Ah, yes . . . 'must be placed in the black bags, clinical in the yellow'. Can't quite work that one out.

Geoff: The hospital waste. It means the paper waste must be placed in the black bags, clinical waste in the yellow bags. It's the waste. Nothing to do with posting things.

Sally: So, have you got any information on the postal service?

Harry: Er . . . looks like it's gone into one of the black bags, I'm afraid Sally . . . Ah, here's something . . . listen to this, all of you. 'The company who collect our paper waste have discovered clinical waste in the wrong bags, which puts their employees at risk, and if it doesn't stop they will refuse to take any waste at all, which means we would have to shut down the hospital.' So, I mean, it's quite clear that this department is to blame. It's all here in black and white. I mean it's terrible, really. Clinical waste in the black bags . . . I hope I don't have to mention that one again. Right then, any questions? Anything we haven't covered . . . *Great*. Meeting over.

Predictably Harry's team are left perplexed, baffled and somewhat uneasy by the incoherence and the generalised ticking off. He has set the stage all right, made sure that everyone can see, hear and be heard without interruption. But has he bothered to plan that there will be anything said worth hearing? Evidently not; but Harry himself is blissfully unaware of the fact as he returns to his room quite a bit chuffed with himself. He finds Mrs Hope, looking somewhat less chuffed.

Harry: Well, basically I thought that went pretty well. We covered a lot of ground and I think everyone now knows where they stand.
Mrs Hope: Really?
Harry: Well, there were no questions anyway.
Mrs Hope: Do you mind if I show you something?

Mrs Hope shows Harry her screen, and he looks on aghast as she plays back the team's reactions.

Sally: I couldn't understand a single word he was on about. I still don't know what's happening with the postal service.

Rebecca: What is the point of these meetings? We may as well stand in a darkened room for half an hour . . .

Geoff: I preferred the old days, when nobody told you anything. At least you knew where you were then . . .

Harry stares at Mrs Hope.

Harry: . . . Well, why didn't they ask questions, then?

Mrs Hope: Mr Willis, we now come to the second stage of talking to your team. **Prepare your script.**

Harry: Script? I haven't got a script.

Mrs Hope: Then write one. First of all, **make a list of the subjects** you want to talk to the team about, and then **group your points** together.

Harry: Well, it's very easy for you to say that, group your points together, but I mean how? Alphabetically? Or start with the little words and work upwards?

Mrs Hope: Simple. Begin with the past: review the team's performance. How did we do last month? Then deal with the present, current problems, new information, on-going projects, time-keeping . . . and finally . . .

Harry: Wait a minute, wait a minute, I think I might get this one . . . the future?

Mrs Hope: Exactly. Forward plans, forthcoming changes, things that are going to affect the team, and that they must prepare for.

Harry: All right. So I make a list of all the points that have to be covered. And then I just read out from my 'script' . . .

Mrs Hope: No, you don't.

Harry: No, I don't. I don't read out from my script.

Mrs Hope: Don't read out from anything. Put it into your own words, **use everyday language**. But above all else, make it **relevant** to the team.

Harry: Relevant? . . . We weren't exactly discussing the origins of Christianity in there, you know.

Mrs Hope: You might as well have been. 'Hospital activity is to go up by five per cent . . .'

Harry: What's wrong with that?

Mrs Hope: What does it mean to the team?

Harry: Well, it means we'll be doing at least three more operations a week.

Mrs Hope: Then say so. People will lose interest fast if you don't make the information relevant to them.

Harry: All right.

Mrs Hope: And third, **anticipate questions** from the team.

Harry: Anticipate questions? Well, unfortunately, unlike you, I'm not a mind-reader.

Mrs Hope: You don't have to be, but, for example, if you've given somebody a form to fill in, it's pretty obvious that they're going to ask what they should do with it when they've finished.

Harry: Yes. Fair enough. So, let's see if I've got this. To prepare my script, I list my points; then I group them together, starting with the past and a review of the team's performance . . . Next I make sure that the information is relevant to the team . . . and finally I anticipate questions from the team.

Mrs Hope: Excellent. Now can you remember all that?

Harry: Child's play.

Once again Harry marches off to the fray, confidently looking forward to the next meeting. This time his team have transmuted themselves into employees of an insurance company. Harry confronts them, notes and agenda before him, and startles them with an alarmingly competent introduction.

Harry: Right, hello everyone. First of all, I'll just run over the list of subjects we're going to be covering this morning. We'll take them one by one, and if we've got time at the end, talk about other points you'd like to raise. Now, I'd like to put you in the picture as regards last month's revenue which has shown a marked increase, and we're going to have to talk about what that means to us as a team; next, the department's acquisition of a laser printer, which I hope is going to make all our lives easier; and finally, I'd just like to run over the suggested arrangements for this year's Christmas party. OK?

The team stares at him open-mouthed. This is not the Harry they have come to know and despise.

Harry: Now then. Last month's revenue was £812,303 which meant that we down here had to cope with more applications than usual for this time of year. 2,000 more in fact, which is something of a record month, all those long working hours and Saturday mornings. Terrific effort all round. There'll be celebration drinks in the conference room on Monday as a way of saying thank you. Now, until such time as we have been able to carry out accurate in-depth market analysis of the down-line probabilities . . . er I mean, well, basically until we know how long it's going to last, we're going to need some help to get through this stage. OK? Yes, Rebecca?

Rebecca: Have we any idea of the reason for this increase?

Harry: Well, it seems to be the result of our very intense national advertising campaign . . .

Bill: 'Intense' is not the word I'd have chosen.

Harry: Sorry, Bill?

Bill: The adverts on TV are rubbish. Complete rubbish.

Harry: Well, I don't know about that, Bill. I think they're pretty good, aren't they?

Sally: I quite like the one about the bishop in the Turkish bath . . .

Bill: This one about a woman playing golf . . .

Geoff: That's the best one.

Harry: Er, right. Perhaps we could leave this . . .

Bill: It's rubbish. Listen. A seventy-five-year-old man would not take a crocodile with him on a round of golf.

Geoff: It's a joke, for heaven's sake!

Arthur: Well, I hate to disagree with . . . er . . . well, with anybody, really. But . . .

Bill: But what?

Geoff: You don't think it's a joke?

Arthur: I think it's an alligator.

Sally: Well, the adverts can't be all that bad if we're selling all these extra insurance products, can they?

Bill: But the reason for that, young Sally, is that the Sales department have just taken on thirty extra staff.

Sally: I didn't know that.

Bill: Oh yes. You've got thirty new staff out there, knocking on people's doors – that's why we've been landed with all this extra work.

Geoff: Is that true?

Bill: Of course it's true. I've just told you.

Geoff: I'd rather hear it from Harry, if it's all the same with you.

All eyes turn on Harry, who, of course, hasn't the faintest idea whether it's true or not.

Harry: Er . . . well . . . er . . . yes, the Sales department have certainly been undergoing a period of restructuring.

Bill: There. Told you.

Rebecca: Then why haven't we been allocated more staff?

Bill: Because the morons in management can't hold two thoughts together in their tiny brains at the same time. Wouldn't occur to them that if you increase sales staff, you've got to increase order-processing staff at the same time.

Geoff: You'd have spotted it, Bill, wouldn't you? Funny how they didn't come down and ask you.

Harry: Oh, now, steady on you two . . .

Rebecca: Look, you've got to admit, it doesn't make much sense to increase one department and not the other.

Harry: Well, yes, actually, I mean it is pretty typical of er . . . that lot upstairs, isn't it, when you think about it. I mean they just seem to think that we can cope with whatever they throw at us. It is stupid, really.

Rebecca: So what are we going to do about it?

Harry: Er . . . 'do'?

Rebecca: Do. How are we going to respond?

Bill: I'd say one of us should go straight up there and make our opinions known.

Harry: Well, let's not rush into . . .

Geoff: What, just walk straight into the boardroom?

Bill: Well, why not? It's the only way to make yourself heard in this flipping place. I think we should take a vote on who goes up.

Geoff: Oh, I notice you're not volunteering, then?

Bill: Me? Why should I?'

Geoff: Well, you're keen enough to do all the talking when we're around.

Bill: I speak my mind, if that's what you mean. There's no crime in that.

Geoff: Almost anything to do with your mind is a crime.

Harry: Look, let's all just CALM DOWN . . .

A distraught Harry closes the meeting and races back to his office where Mrs Hope is waiting.

Harry: What happened? They wouldn't listen to me.

Mrs Hope: Yes, and why? Because you lost control of the meeting.

Harry: . . . Slightly.

Mrs Hope: And that's because you now need to learn a third and final lesson: **control your audience**. You see, the greatest single thing that gives you control is preparation. The more you've thought things out, the more you can control the audience. Then, once you have prepared, **don't let anyone distract you** from the point.

Harry: I didn't. I kept exactly to the script!

Mrs Hope: Really? So a discussion of the company's television advertising campaign was one of your points, was it?

Harry: That wasn't my fault. Bill raised that one!

Mrs Hope: No, he didn't. You were the one who turned it into a discussion by saying you didn't think they were all that bad.

Harry: Well they're not.

Mrs Hope: But that's *irrelevant*. By saying that to Bill you were suddenly inviting everyone to volunteer their opinions on a completely irrelevant subject. You were distracted, and so you gave away control of the meeting.

Harry: Well, perhaps there's something in that.

Mrs Hope: Now, let me ask you something. After preparation, what is your best weapon of control, when running a meeting?

Harry: A flame-thrower?

Mrs Hope: After preparation, your next best weapon is time.

Harry: I beg your pardon?

Mrs Hope: Always suggest that time is precious. Because if you can **keep the momentum** of the meeting going, you'll carry the team along with you. Instead of them carrying you.

Harry: Yes, fine, but that wouldn't have stopped the whole thing about the Sales department having taken on more staff.

Mrs Hope: Have the Sales department taken on more staff?

Harry: Well . . . I don't know.

Mrs Hope: Then, why didn't you say so? If you tell them you don't know the answer, but you'll certainly find out and get back to them as soon as possible, what happens?

Harry: We . . . carry on with the meeting?

Mrs Hope: Exactly. Not so terrible. Now what, do you suppose, is the final lesson?

Harry: The final lesson?

Mrs Hope: Yes.

Harry: I don't know. But I'll certainly find out and get back to you as soon as possible.

Mrs Hope: Support the management.

Harry: Oh, now, come on, everyone else was having a go at management.

Mrs Hope: But you're not everyone else. You're in charge. And who put you there?

Harry: Management.

Mrs Hope: Right, so by undermining the position of management, you undermine . . . ?

Harry: Myself.

Mrs Hope: Exactly. No matter how unpopular the issue, you must present management's case.

Harry: Right, so to control my audience, I have to resist distractions. I have to keep the momentum of the meeting going . . . and above all, I must support the management.

Harry rushes off, all his lessons learned and he is ready to apply them. The meeting convenes . . .

Harry: . . . So, hopefully, the laser printer is going to considerably speed up the turnaround process for policies.

Bill: I don't suppose any training's been organised for the people who are going to have to operate this contraption.

Harry: Training. That's a good point, Bill. I'll find out about that.

Bill: I mean . . . training is quite important.

Harry: Oh absolutely. Now, we'll shortly be having some new people joining us from Investments. Things are a little quiet over there at the moment and so it's a good way of getting us through this extra workload.

Rebecca: Why are Investments so quiet then?

Bill: Because they're bone idle, that's why. I mean, they sit around, scratching their crystal balls, trying to work out whether the Chinese grapefruit market is going up or down . . .

Harry: OK, we're a bit short of time so . . .

Bill: Well, it makes me sick, quite frankly, to see that lot through there . . .

Harry: I *really* think we ought to get on and talk about the Christmas party . . .

Bill: . . . prancing around as if they own the place . . .

Harry: So, do we want it to be like last year's?

Sally: No!

Rebecca: Absolutely not.

Bill: Thinking they're the cat's whiskers. Lord knows why.

Sally: Bill . . . *please*.

Rebecca: I think we'd all rather talk about the Christmas party.

Harry: Yes, Bill, if you don't mind, we really are getting a bit short of time.

Bill: Oh all right then. If you have to talk about the wretched cheese fondue, then be my guest.

Harry: Right. Well, it was generally felt that last year's effort wasn't too successful.

Arthur: I rather enjoyed myself.

Harry: Yes, that was hideously apparent, Arthur, so this year we feel that the best way of . . .

Bill: Hold on a minute. Who is 'we'?

Harry: 'We' are the management, Bill.

The lessons have been well learned. No distractions, plenty of momentum, a clever identification with management. Harry returns in triumph to Mrs Hope who has packed her screen and is getting ready to depart.

Mrs Hope: Congratulations, Mr Willis.

Harry: Thank you, Mrs Hope.

Mrs Hope: All went well?

Harry: Extremely well, thank you. And, if you don't mind I'll tell you why.

Mrs Hope: Please do.

Harry: Because this time I set the stage. I gave everybody advance notice of the meeting, so everybody was there. I organised seating . . . and I avoided interruptions.

Mrs Hope: Not so difficult after all. And then?

Harry: Then, I prepared my script.

Mrs Hope: You grouped your points. Beautifully,

if I may say so. And you reviewed the team's performance as well as making the information relevant to the team.

Harry: And I anticipated questions from the team. And finally, Mrs Hope, I kept control of my audience, I kept the momentum going, and . . . I supported the management. All in all, Mrs Hope, I have the strange feeling I may have just talked to my team. And stranger still, that they may have listened.

Golden rules

1 Always set the stage.
2 Prepare an agenda and have the relevant documents to hand.
3 Create a structure; for example, deal with a review of the past, the present, and future plans if appropriate.
4 Use everyday language.
5 Have the courage to admit not knowing the answer to a question.
6 Control the momentum of your meeting and don't allow irrelevance, especially from yourself.
7 Support the management.

4 How am I doing? The dreaded appraisal

Do you, as a manager, keep your staff in the dark about their performance? Do they know what *you* think of them? As an employee, does your boss find time to tell you how he feels about your work – does he *know* about

it, your most important achievements, or failures? Many companies have an annual appraisal interview designed specifically for this purpose. Unfortunately they can turn out to be worse than useless. Take the experience of Alan Ames, who has had the misfortune to work for each of those three enemies of society: Ethelred the Unready,

Ivan the Terrible and William the Silent. It all comes back to him during another annual event – his regular medical check-up.

> **Dr Evans:** Nice to see you again, Alan. How are you?
>
> **Ames:** Fine.
>
> **Dr Evans:** Good. Sit down. I'm all for these annual get-togethers; if there's anything slightly wrong, we can nip it in the bud. So . . . how are things?
>
> **Ames:** Great. I left that company, Parks and Gibb. I'm with a new firm.
>
> **Dr Evans:** Same sort of work?
>
> **Ames:** Yes, but it's like being in the daylight after five years in the dark. I know what I have to do; I know where I fit in. I mean, when I think back to that lot . . . Nobody ever listened to you, nobody told you what you had to do. You felt so helpless. The good people left because there wasn't enough in their jobs to keep them there, and the bad people stayed put because nobody found them out. I mean, you'd think it was in *their* interest to get the *best* out of them, wouldn't you? Give 'em work they can do and enjoy, or train 'em if they can't. I mean, that's the bloody *problem*!!!
>
> **Dr Evans:** Careful! I've got to take your blood pressure in a moment.
>
> **Ames:** Sorry, but it still gets to me.
>
> **Dr Evans:** But why was it so bad?
>
> **Ames:** Because you never got a **chance to really talk to your boss about your job**. Were you happy, was **he** happy, about how were things going? As simple as that.
>
> **Dr Evans:** But you saw each other every day.

Ames: But that's like those people in your waiting room. You've got a lot of them to see every day. Those are the daily running problems. You haven't got time to give every one of those a full medical check-up.

Dr Evans: No, but I can always arrange a special session like this.

Ames: Yes, *you* can. But we had those. Oh yes. The annual appraisal interviews. They were the salt in the wound. You went in raw; you came out bleeding. I can still remember one when I was in Sales under Ethelred. I'd really done jolly well that year. Worked flat out for weeks on a big overseas order. I was expecting a pat on the back.

Alan recalls the occasion bitterly.

Ethelred: Alan . . . Oh yes, annual interview.

Ames: Annual interview? I didn't know about this.

Ethelred: Yes, you remember. The Personnel department in its wisdom decrees that we should have an annual interview.

Ames: When?

Ethelred: Well, I thought we could knock it off now.

Ames: Now?

Ethelred: Why not?

Ames: Well, I'd like to have done a bit of thinking . . .

Ethelred: Yes, well the only thing is I've got a bit behind with them. I've got three this morning *and* lunch with the Chairman. Look, this is only a formality. I mean, we see each other every day anyway. So . . . everything going OK?

Ames: Well, let's talk about it. Anywhere in particular you'd like to start?

Ethelred: No. Nowhere in particular, no. No complaints. A pity about the mess-up over the relaunch of the PX 20. Still, you can't win 'em all.

Ames: But I wasn't working on the relaunch.

Ethelred: Weren't you? Well, never mind. Set us back three months that did.

Ames: Yes, but I had nothing to do with that.

Ethelred: No, right . . . Been on any courses this year?

Ames: No.

Ethelred: Well, you should know. What about the new product range appreciation course, for instance?

Ames: Well, that was the course I asked to go on at this interview last year.

Ethelred: Oh did you? Oh well, good idea then. *Last* year's interview? I must take a look at that some time. Or of course there's a language course. But you don't speak any languages, do you?

Ames: Yes, I'm fairly fluent in French and German.

Ethelred: What?

Ames: It's on my file.

Ethelred: Yes, yes, I'm sure it is. Wish we'd known when the Frankfurt people were over here on the PX launch. On no, you weren't involved with that.

Ames: No! I wasn't.

Ethelred: I thought . . . Oh, well, never mind. Now, we don't seem to be getting much general customer information from you.

Ames: Hell, I write up my report sheets.

Ethelred: No, I mean the sort of general customer feedback for the marketing people.

Ames: Surely that's not my responsibility, is it?

Ethelred: Yes!

Ames: It wasn't in my job description.

Ethelred: Wasn't it? Well, I mean, you can't be *too* rigid about that. Personnel department bumph. I mean you've got to take it with a pinch of salt. Anyway the main thing is to make sure you do it in the future. OK?

Ames: Yes, but you've never mentioned that I hadn't been doing it before.

Ethelred: No. Well, I mean, that's what these annual interviews are for, isn't it? Pick up the mistakes that haven't been mentioned during the year. Anything else? Oh, yes, you're nearly due for a salary review. We could knock that off too while you're here. Now, you'll be getting the general increase next month. OK?

Ames: Well, I wondered if I wasn't due a bit more than an ordinary rise.

Ethelred: Well, there are a lot of chaps older than you on the same scale, Alan.

Ames: You mean I'm not worth any more?

Ethelred: Alan, you know me. I'd double everyone's salary if I could . . .

Ames: Look, have you talked to Les Strudwick about my Iranian presentation?

Ethelred: Not as such, no.

Ames: It went very well.

Ethelred: Yes, well. I agree he hasn't complained.

Ames: Complained! We got the order!

Ethelred: Yes. Well, as I said, Alan, generally I've got no complaint . . .

Ames: *No complaint*!

Ethelred: As far as I know, no.

Ames: What do you mean, you've got no complaint 'as far as you know'? I mean, how can we discuss a complaint if you don't know whether you've got one

or not. Look, what about the Iranian order?
Ethelred: Yes, well. That was jolly good. Jolly good.
You were on that . . . ?

Ethelred the Unready probably has the family motto 'Be Unprepared'. Among the many things he has not bothered to think about are:

1 That an appraisal interview is important
2 That it requires elementary courtesies such as due notice with the right balance between formality and informality
3 That both parties need time for preparation

Having failed in this, the rest of the débâcle followed naturally. Ethelred should have thought through what the employee needed from the interview and realised that the same information was necessary to him as manager to make his appraisal. Broadly, what both parties need is an answer to the questions:

1 What is expected?
2 How am I doing?
3 Where am I going?
4 What can I do to improve?

Needless to say, Ethelred gave himself no chance to explore these, let alone **prepare** them against the background of a job description, standards of performance expected, any specific targets set and short-term priority tasks to be performed. He has naturally never considered that appraisal should fill a vital link between the company and the employee; that it is in the employee's, manager's and company's interest to:

1 Review progress and priorities
2 Resolve problems arising in these areas

3 Discuss the employee's potential and future
   training needs

In other words, the appraisal interview should be a
dialogue and the employee should leave the interview
with a clear idea of the manager's response to the
question 'How am I doing?' The manager needs an
equally clear idea!

Recounting his experience, Ames gives a pithy summary of Ethelred's failings to Dr Evans:

> **Ames:** He just hadn't taken the trouble to find out
> the first thing about me. Didn't even tell me I was
> going to have an annual interview and give me time
> to think about it. Hadn't talked to the *Export
> Manager* about the work I'd done for him . . . didn't
> have the record of my previous interview. Didn't
> have my job description. Hadn't looked at my
> personal file. Our one big chat of the year and he
> hadn't done five minutes' homework on it. Just not
> interested. Typical of the whole bloody company . . .
> **Dr Evans:** You know, I was just thinking what it
> would be like if a doctor started behaving like that at
> a check-up. I mean, think of Ethelred as a doctor.
> Think about it . . .
>
> **Dr Ethelred:** Ah, Mr Ames, do sit down.
> **Ames:** Thank you.
> **Dr Ethelred:** Well, well. I haven't seen you since . . .
> **Ames:** The operation.
> **Dr Ethelred:** What? No, no, no. I've seen you since
> then. That was two years ago.
> **Ames:** No it wasn't.
> **Dr Ethelred:** Yes it was. I went straight in after I'd
> got back from Spain.

Ames: No, no – my operation.

Dr Ethelred: Oh, *yours*. You've had an operation?

Ames: Yes! Last month.

Dr Ethelred: Ah. Did you . . . enjoy it?

Ames: What?

Dr Ethelred: How is it . . . now?

Ames: Better.

Dr Ethelred: Good, good, good. That's what we doctors are here for.

Ames: . . . It was the heart transplant.

Dr Ethelred: Mr Ames? . . . Well, well, well, I was thinking it was Mr Adams . . . and it was you. Well, I'd better take him off your pills . . . pronto. Well, how are things . . . in general, apart from . . . the heart?

Ames: Fine. Not bad. I still get these headaches occasionally.

Dr Ethelred: Well, we've got something that'll get rid of those immediately. Marvellous new stuff called Anti-paracetin . . .

Ames: Dr Marsh has just taken me off those.

Dr Ethelred: Did he?

Ames: Yes, he said I had an aspirin allergy.

Dr Ethelred: Ah, well. In that case best avoid them.

Ames: Isn't this on my record? He said it could be fatal . . . with the . . .

Dr Ethelred: . . . the heart, yes, but only relatively fatal. Only in the strict medical sense. Yes, ah, here's the card. Eyesight still OK?

Ames: Yes.

Dr Ethelred: Good. Any after-affects from the hysterectomy?

Ames: What?

Dr Ethelred: Hasn't it been depressing lately . . .

Yes, that's exactly how Ethelred would approach his responsibilities to a patient. In fact, there are a great many similarities between the good doctor and the good manager. People's careers are vital to them – so is their health. Both are worth a little homework on an occasion

like the annual interview. Just as the doctor has to review the patient's case history in advance of the check-up, so the manager must do the same. In short, he must know what he's talking about. Equally, however, he mustn't do *all* the talking. Alan recalls a memorable interview when he worked in Central Sales under Ivan the Terrible . . .

> **Ivan:** Right. Well, as you know, this is the annual appraisal interview, where the company tells you what it thinks of you. There's your assessment . . .

plenty of room for improvement, as I think you'll agree.

Ames: Look, I'm sorry. I don't really understand this. What's this BB – for efficiency? How do you calculate this sort of thing?

Ivan: I don't have to calculate. I know.

Ames: Yes. But I . . .

Ivan: You fly by the seat of your pants, Alan. You've got good instincts – but when it comes down to the detail, you won't get down to it.

Ames: But there are several other things . . .

Ivan: I know your sort, Alan. I've had plenty of experience of them.

Ames: Yes, but I don't accept that I'm inefficient.

Ivan: I'm telling you, you are inefficient.

Ames: Well, where's your evidence?

Ivan: Evidence? Come on, Alan . . . You don't like criticism, that's your trouble.

Ames: Look, if you mean the order office . . .

Ivan: Yes I do. It's a mess.

Ames: It's the way it's organised. Look, I've written out a new procedure.

Ivan: I hardly think this is the time . . .

Ames: But you're usually very busy, it's terribly difficult to get to see you.

Ivan: Well, I'm a busy man. I have to run a department that's responsible for . . .

Ames: Exactly. But *now* we've got some time together . . . I mean this new procedure is absolutely central to my job. This is what I'm supervising. At the moment we send out first an order acknowledgement, then an invoice, then some pay when we send on the statement. Some even pay twice. The girls are bogged down in paper and they spend ages reconciling cheques and statements. What I suggest is that for all normal orders we send out just one document instead of three – a combined acknowledgement, invoice and statement.

Ivan: Look, Alan, this is just proving my point. You can't take criticism.

Ames: I *can* take criticism.

Ivan: No you can't. I'm criticising you now, aren't I? And you're arguing. You're obstinate. You have to blame it all on someone else – it's the system. It's the company, you'll be saying next.

Ames: I am not blaming the company. I was merely trying to improve the way we do things.

Ivan: Right. And I'm trying to improve the way *you* do things, Alan. You're so bloody busy telling everyone else where they're going wrong, you never stop and look at your own faults. Well, that's what this interview is *for* . . .

In many ways Ivan's results resemble those of Ethelred's. Ames has no idea how he is doing because neither has thought through the interview from the employee's point of view. Needless to say, neither has created the opportunity for a dialogue. Ivan, if he wasn't so terrible, would benefit from learning the classic interview style of *open-ended* questions, those which avoid yes and no answers and which are geared to getting facts and opinions from the interviewee. For example:

What was the most interesting task you had to do this year?

What was your most successful area in the past year?

How do you feel you handled the reorganisation in retrospect?

What areas of your work would you say require more attention?

What extra help do you need to improve those areas?

What do you think you need to learn now to develop the job further?

How have you found dealings with Accounts and Marketing have worked out?

What have been the most difficult problems you have faced?

Where do you see your future in the company?

How do you see this job developing?

What would you say are the priorities for the next twelve months?

Such questions do not fit the Ivan style which goes by instinct and, of course, believes in reaching the conclusion before the evidence. His is a type not too impressed by factual information as Ames, finishing his recollection of the unhappy episode, explains to Dr Evans . . .

Ames: See what I mean? You couldn't get through. There was no **discussion of facts** . . .

Dr Evans: Yes, I can imagine Ivan as a doctor . . .

Dr Ivan: You've got a nasty pain there.

Ames: Where?

Dr Ivan: There.

Ames: . . . No I haven't.

Dr Ivan: Nasty pain.

Ames: Really I *haven't* got a pain there.

Dr Ivan: Now, now. *Who's* the doctor? Have you got medical qualifications? No? Right. On the scales . . . You're a foot too short!

Ames: What?

Dr Ivan: You're a foot too short!

Ames: You mean at this weight I ought to be a foot taller.

Dr Ivan: Definitely.

Ames: Well, then, I ought to lose weight.

Dr Ivan: You ought to, but you won't.

Ames: Why not?

Dr Ivan: I know your type. You over-eat and won't take exercise.

Ames: But I would . . .

Dr Ivan: I don't know what to do with you – if I give you a diet, you won't stick to it. If I give you exercises, you won't do them.

Ames: I'll do jogging.

> **Dr Ivan:** If I give you pills, you won't take them.
> **Ames:** I would! I would! I promise you I would.
> **Dr Ivan:** And I'm telling you you wouldn't.
> **Ames:** . . . Wouldn't I?
> **Dr Ivan:** You wouldn't.
> **Ames:** Isn't there anything we can do?
> **Dr Ivan:** No, nothing. It's hopeless . . . you'd best
> have your coronary now, while I'm here to deal with
> it. Well, come on, come on, we haven't got all day.

Once again, the similarities between the doctor and the manager are demonstrated. The doctor should only discuss those things which can be remedied or improved. It is no good discussing an employee's personality defects (as you see them) with him. You discuss results and performance. 'You don't have an aptitude for detail' is no more a management appraisal without facts and discussion of those facts than 'You are too short' is a medical opinion. When a doctor discusses a weight problem it is, or should be, as a problem, not as a criticism. Work difficulties can be diagnosed just as conscientiously as illnesses; and the response is more likely to be a good one if the tone of the exchange is helpful. Remember, when you are finding fault, to acknowledge successes as well. A doctor who says, 'I'm pleased with your weight loss, and I can see you are trying, but let's see if we can manage a little more,' will make more progress than one who simply says, 'You're too fat.' And never formulate your opinion, diagnosis or conclusion *before* you have both the necessary information and have given the employee an opportunity to explain points which may be relevant.

Alan's last appraisal interview was with William the Silent. As he tells Dr Evans, William was a nice enough person who listened, had done his homework but had one terrible fault. By the time of that interview Alan was pretty fed up with the whole company . . .

William: Right, well. I'll arrange for you to go on that course then. And you want a spell away from line management some time . . .
Ames: Soon.
William: Yes, right, jolly good, OK. Well, very pleased you can . . . speak out like this, jolly healthy.
Ames: Are you satisfied with me?
William: . . . Sorry?
Ames: Are you satisfied with me?
William: Oh yes. Yes, yes, yes. Er . . . Well, there is one . . . small thing . . .
Ames: What?
William: Well . . . the letter you wrote to the *Gazette*.
Ames: What was wrong with it?
William: Oh, it was just, well, it was, you know, well, a bit critical of our industry.
Ames: So you don't think firms like ours have a pollution problem?
William: Oh yes, oh yes. But don't you think 'capitalist rip-off' was a bit . . . strong?
Ames: It's true, isn't it?
William: Well, yes, yes, yes. It's a point of view, certainly . . .
Ames: *My* point of view.
William: Yes, exactly . . . but . . . if you'd written it from your home address rather than on company paper . . . ?
Ames: It's only coming from a named company that gives it any authority. Don't you think it's time this country woke up to the environmental facts of life?

William: Yes . . . Oh yes.

Ames: Unless the people who know have the guts to speak out, things will get worse and worse, won't they?

William: Er, yes. Right.

Ames: Well, there you are. We've agreed on something.

William: . . . Yes, I, er, I think I ought just to make a teeny mention of it in the report. Just, you know . . .

Ames: No.

William: Just a note? . . . Just a small . . . I know the Chairman felt . . .

Ames: Look, who's interviewing me – the Chairman or you?

William: I am. And I do feel that . . .

Ames: Fine. So long as I can write again to the *Gazette* saying you've officially censured me for telling the truth.

William: . . . Well, I suppose we could sort of unofficially record it . . . gentleman's agreement . . .

Ames: All right. So long as nothing goes in the report.

William: No . . . right.

William is a 'ducker', the type of manager who will not face up to things. Here there has been no **discussion of performance**, just an ill-judged attempt to raise one isolated and specific criticism which of its nature just does not belong to an annual appraisal anyway unless it can be put in the context of an overall approach or attitude to the job.

William should have been less silent on Ames's standards of performance. He should have asked himself, if Ames's standards had turned out to be well in excess of what was expected:

1 Whether the standards were too low
2 He was just a fantastic manager
3 How he was going to be developed
4 If luck, such as unexpected market trends, had contributed to performance

And if performance fell short of standards:

1 Whether standards were too high
2 If there were company factors (including you, the boss) which were less than helpful
3 Whether training or guidance was necessary
4 What you, as manager, were going to do about it

Yes, there is no point in avoiding issues. The appraisal interview is, in effect, a check-up for both manager and employee. It *must* conclude on a positive note for the future, even if that positive note is some form of follow-up of a weakness. For this reason notes on the appraisal *must* be taken, a summary sent or a form filled in for Personnel, and some use made of it at intervals during the year so that progress can be monitored. It is part of the manager's job to keep employees informed about their progress and in this area silence is never a virtue.

Nor would silence be a virtue in a doctor who is supposed to give opinions, not receive them. As Alan comes to the end of his experience of William, Dr Evans has no difficulty imagining what kind of doctor he would make . . .

> **Ames:** What do you mean, overweight?
> **Dr William:** . . . Well, nothing, nothing.
> **Ames:** Good. Now shut up.
> **Dr William:** Yes, but . . . well, let me put it this way, your blood pressure is a bit high.

Ames: So?
Dr William: Well . . . I mean it's, to be blunt . . . it's phenomenally high.
Ames: I *like* it phenomenally high!

No good doctor shirks his responsibilities; nor does a good manager. They check case histories, collect information, make a diagnosis, discuss it as appropriate – and finally **agree a plan of action**. Ethelred could have *no* plan of action through lack of forethought; Ivan would give a hectoring and irrelevant lecture on restructuring his employee's personality; and William would avoid action through weakness and a desire to avoid any possibility of unpleasantness. Where faults exist, recognise them, bring them out into the open and give yourself every chance to agree a plausible plan for improvement with your employee. Make it a *plausible* plan. Remember that you are looking for improvements which you may get, not sainthood which you won't. Tell an overweight businessman to jog for ten minutes a day and he'll probably do it. Tell him to run five miles and he'll stay in bed. Always follow up the agreed plan at regular intervals – don't leave it for next year's annual appraisal interview. And make a report immediately following the interview – then you'll have it properly recorded when next year comes round, and something to consult *through the year* as you check on the progress of the various items you have agreed.

Golden rules

1 Remember appraisal is important to those concerned.
2 Prepare properly and check relevant job descriptions, standards and targets.
3 The interviewee *must* leave the interview knowing the answer to 'How Am I Doing?'
4 Appraisal should be a two-way dialogue.
5 Use open questions to explore difficulties.
6 Agree plans for improvement where appropriate and how they are to be monitored.

5 I'd like a word with you – the discipline interview

According to the *Oxford English Dictionary*, discipline means, among other things, 'correction; chastisement; punishment . . . the mortification of the flesh by penance'. Possibly when you are in a bad mood this definition has a certain appeal. But for managers it is the other definitions from the dictionary which are more relevant:

1 Instructions imparted to disciples or scholars; teaching; learning; education; schooling
2 Instruction having for its aim to form the pupil to proper conduct and action

You can think of discipline in business as a combination of two things, one static and one dynamic. Static discipline is about having a clear and fair framework within which everyone can work: clear and fair rules on smoking, safety, timekeeping, and so on – and agreed standards of work for employees. Dynamic discipline is about ensuring that the rules and standards are kept and, if they are not, taking action to close the gap between required performance and actual performance.

Gaps like this can open up for a number of reasons: because the rules are so outdated that no one bothers with them; or because the rules and standards were never communicated to an employee – so ignorance is innocence, even if it is not bliss; or because someone chooses to flout the prescribed framework.

In the first instance the remedy is for management to take urgent action to revise and update its procedures and regulations; in the second, to look hard at its internal communications. But in the last case it is down to you, the individual's boss, to sort out the situation. So, before you know what's happened, you find yourself conducting a discipline interview, whether you meant to or not, and whether or not you call it by that name.

It is usually one of three things that sparks off a discipline interview:

1. For some managers the need becomes obvious as a result of a logical analysis of someone's behaviour or performance against the accepted standards of his job.
2. For other managers it may be a simple relay action – your boss bawls you out for a mess-up on a particular project, so you decide to pass on his words, suitably amplified, to the individual who messed it up.

You pass on the boss's words, suitably amplified, to the individual who messed it up

3 The third reason is that something snaps inside you, and you realise that you can't stomach Harry's abusiveness or Joan's lateness any longer, and that they are not responding to your 'hey, watch your language' or 'see you on time tomorrow' remarks.

If you are the type of person who falls into the first category, you can congratulate yourself. You have a greater chance of getting the interview off on the right foot. If you have found yourself in the second or third categories, beware! Remember the adage about fools rushing in. Your temper and instant response to a situation will probably cause trouble. Temper breeds aggression in others – therefore a satisfactory conversation is unlikely. Also, if you instantly leap into an interview you will be breaking the first cardinal rule of interviewing: be prepared.

If you are in a temper you are quite likely to forgo the refinements of privacy and bawl the person out in front of others. However wrong the person is, all you are doing is making a martyr out of him and a fool of yourself in front of the rest of the staff. So before you say that pregnant phrase, 'I'd like a word with you . . .', what should you do?

First and foremost, remember that future performance is your real concern, so keep the bulk of the interview pointing forward and avoid excessive argument and recrimination about the past.

Next, think of yourself as trying to repair a gap, the gap between someone's required performance and his actual performance. There are three stages to a discipline interview:

1 Establishing the gap
2 Exploring the reasons for the gap
3 Eliminating the gap

Let's take **establishing the gap** first. That's the part that defeats our old friend Ethelred the Unready. Here he is, unprepared as carefully as always, ready to take issue with George who is not really pulling his weight and needs to become aware of the fact . . .

> **Ethelred:** George, come in and sit down. Now then, let me tell you what this is about . . . as soon as I've found your time-sheets. Susan must have filed them. Now . . . oh, we need your job cards, don't we . . . there we are. Now George, you're not really pulling your weight, are you? Look at the figures.
>
> **George:** What's wrong with them?
>
> **Ethelred:** These time-sheets and job cards aren't filled out properly. They're very important, we can't schedule calls . . .
>
> **George:** I didn't know they mattered.
>
> **Ethelred:** Of course they matter. What do you think we have them for? Look at that one – it's got beer stains all over it. I mean, it's obviously concocted in a pub, isn't it?
>
> **George:** Where do you want me to do them, in church? I didn't know you cared so much about the bloody forms. I thought it was better to get on with the job. But if you want me to fill in the forms, I'll fill in the forms! But you've never mentioned it before, have you?
>
> **Ethelred:** Not as such, perhaps. But I should have thought it was obvious that we couldn't schedule . . .
>
> **George:** Well it isn't. When old Harry was the supervisor, he didn't care about the forms.

> **Ethelred:** Well I didn't know that, did I?

First point: in order to establish the gap between standards and performance you must check the facts on the standard for the job. Then you have another pitfall to avoid:

> **Ethelred:** I'm sorry George, but your call rate's not up to standard.
> **George:** What standard? How many calls do the others make, then?
> **Ethelred:** Well, I don't know the exact figures. But look at this . . . completely blank.
> **George:** That was the afternoon you called us in for a meeting. Next?
> **Ethelred:** How about that! One call in the whole day?
> **George:** The job took all day, didn't it!
> **Ethelred:** Look, the point is, I *know* your call rate's not good enough. I'm going to give you a warning.
> **George:** And I'm going to talk to my shop steward.

Second point: as well as checking on standards, you also have to check on performance. Otherwise you can't establish that there's a gap between them. But suppose Ethelred had done his homework . . .

> **Ethelred:** George, is there any reason that these time-sheets and job cards are not filled in properly?
> **George:** Better to do the job than waste the day filling in forms.
> **Ethelred:** But we waste time if we can't schedule the calls properly. And we can't schedule if we don't know which jobs have been done. We can't send the bills either.
> **George:** Old Harry never seemed bothered about it.

Ethelred: That's one of the things we've got to put right. From now on these forms must be accurately completed.

George: I don't forget very often.

Ethelred: Well, actually you do. Less than half of these are properly filled in.

George: None of the lads bother about them.

Ethelred: That's partly true, but they're all better than this. I've been through all the time-sheets and yours definitely contain the least information.

George: I do the job all right though, don't I?

Ethelred: You could be one of our best engineers, but your call rate is a bit low. Tell me, is there any reason why you never call in after three o'clock for unallocated calls?

George: My allocated calls take all day.

Ethelred: Always?

George: Nearly always.

Ethelred: Every housewife is nearly always in when you call? You see, if you don't do your full quota it puts extra strain on everybody else. Do you see what I mean? We'll say no more about it, because you may have thought I was happy with Harry's system. So this is just an informal warning. But in future these time-sheets and job cards must be completely accurate. Otherwise I shall have to give you a formal warning.

George: I'll talk to my shop steward.

Ethelred: That's fine. All these procedures are agreed with the union. But you just have to do this and there's nothing to worry about.

So that's it. He had the facts on the standards of the job. He had the facts on the actual performance. So it was possible to be very specific about the gap between the two.

Now let's look at another old friend, Ivan the Terrible. His weak point is **exploring the reasons for the gap**.

> **Ivan:** Ah, there you are Joan. Late again.
>
> **Joan:** I'm sorry but . . .
>
> **Ivan:** Well sorry's no good, is it? This is the third time in two weeks. The company doesn't exist for your convenience, you know. Everyone else gets here on time. Look! All here, working away. Doing your work as well as theirs. It's not fair, is it?
>
> **Joan:** No, but . . .
>
> **Ivan:** No, it's not fair. What have you got to say for yourself?
>
> **Joan:** Nothing.
>
> **Ivan:** Nothing? Well, if you turn up late again you needn't bother to come back.

To start with, you should never reprimand people 'off the cuff'. The best approach is to fix a time to see the person concerned, saying you want to discuss his or her work, time-keeping or whatever, and ensure that the meeting is conducted in private. The discipline interview is not a spectator sport, and nosy-parkers won't help either of you to resolve the situation. Constant interruptions can give the person concerned the idea that you are not really bothered, and that in any case you are too busy to care.

Fixing a time means that your temper can cool, and you can prepare yourself before the interview. Don't put things off indefinitely, though; breaches of discipline should be discussed within twenty-four hours of the event.

The discipline interview is not a specatator sport

Your initial approach is crucial. Apart from being clear about the facts, you must constantly remind yourself to stick to them. Stay calm and don't allow any prejudice or animosity to show. Because of his irritation with her, Ivan has almost sacked Joan, who has been a good worker for years. That's why it's so important to explore the reasons for the gap . . . Why was Joan late? Can Ivan repair the damage?

> **Ivan:** Now, Joan, perhaps I was a bit short with you this morning. I didn't really give you a chance to speak, did I? Well, now's your chance.
> **Joan:** Well, you see, I . . .
> **Ivan:** I'm like that sometimes. I jump down people's throats. I don't mean to but I do. I know I do. I

bloody well *terrify* some of them . . . Well, come on
Joan, get on with it!

Joan: What do you want me to say?

Ivan: Why are you behaving so irresponsibly lately?
Well not . . . but why are you letting us down?
Behaving so badly?

The exploration must be a real one. That means asking
open questions, not loaded ones. Open questions are the
ones that invite a full explanation, rather than a short,
defensive reply. They are particularly useful when dealing with sullen, silent types. Just ask your question and
shut up. By the normal rules of conversation you will get
an answer, even if the answer does take some time to
come out.

From your homework you will have the facts of the
case, but a discipline interview is not just a one-sided
conversation, a 'show trial'. The person must be encouraged to state his case and you must attempt to create an
atmosphere in which he will do this. Don't jump to the
conclusion that you are dealing with a discipline problem
in the first place. Keep your mind open – then the
questions will be too. Let's look at Ivan approaching the
problem properly.

Ivan: Ah, Joan, there you are.

Joan: I'm sorry, but . . . I can't cope . . .

Ivan: Now, what's the trouble?

Joan: I'll go and start work.

Ivan: No, I want to know *why* you're late.

Joan: I'm tired.

Ivan: Yes? . . .

Joan: Well . . . I live with my old mum, and I look
after her without any help, but the week before last
she had a nasty fall. She's eighty-one, you know, and

she can't be left alone. I don't want her to go to a home so I arranged for a home help to come every morning at eight o'clock, but sometimes she's late and I have to wait for her.

Ivan: Yes. Well, you sort things out at home, and if you have to be a bit late a few mornings, we'll manage for a bit.

By listening, Ivan has discovered that this *isn't really a discipline problem at all*. Which gives him the option of adjusting, for a time, the standards he expects of Joan.

So when you're exploring the reasons for the gap, don't jump to conclusions. One, ask open questions. Two, listen patiently for the answers and three, check that it really is a discipline problem. If you do make exceptions, *make sure you tell the others*.

Finally, **eliminate the gap.** That's William the Silent's big problem. He sees the situation as a struggle for dominance – and he's frightened he's going to lose. He has a problem with Jonathan . . .

Jonathan: You wanted to see me?
William: Er . . . yes. Well, how are things?
Jonathan: Fine, how's things with you?
William: Yes . . . fine.
Jonathan: So we're both fine. Is there anything else? I'm fairly busy at the moment.
William: Well, just a couple of things that I ought to mention.
Jonathan: What?
William: I'm coming to them. Now in my position as Acting Head of Sales, I have to . . . thank you for coming here . . . especially as this is in the nature of a dis . . . dis . . .

Jonathan: Dis what?

William: . . . Discipline interview. Well, not exactly discipline, but I mean . . . er . . . we're all grown men, but rules are rules.

Jonathan: Are you saying that I'm not doing my job properly?

William: Would you like a coffee?

William is blurring everything by turning it into a 'who's in charge?' struggle. He should focus on the facts. But that is not everything . . .

Jonathan: You wanted to see me?

William: Yes. Just about a couple of things.

Jonathan: I'm very busy at the moment.

William: You seem to be er . . . overspending your budget.

Jonathan: How do you mean?

William: Your budget is over the . . . how shall I say it? . . . spent. It's supposed to be £100,000 per quarter. But last quarter you spent over £120,000.

Jonathan: That's all right. My sales have gone up 20 per cent.

William: I beg your pardon?

Jonathan: My budget was allocated as 25 per cent of the expected sales. My sales have gone up 20 per cent.

William: But your budget is expressed as a figure, not as a percentage of sales.

Jonathan: It's all very well for you people up there in your penthouse suites. You just sit here shuffling papers around. My salesmen are down there making money for the company.

William: I do know a bit about it, you know – I was in Sales for six years. And now that I'm Acting Head

of Sales, well . . . I'm in charge. I'd like to make this
perfectly clear . . .

William has focused on the facts all right but has not
stuck to them. He has allowed himself to be diverted
from a perfectly reasonable point and to become distracted by what is essentially irrelevant. Let us look at
how he *should* have dealt with things:

> **William:** Jonathan, the point is that you spent
> £120,000 instead of £100,000.
> **Jonathan:** Yes, but I think my budget should be
> expressed in percentage terms.
> **William:** That's not the way this company works.
> **Jonathan:** It's the way I work.
> **William:** Are you saying that you can't work with
> this company?
> **Jonathan:** No, I didn't mean that.
> **William:** We work to agreed budgets. We have a set
> of agreed standards which you accepted when you
> joined us, didn't you? So either you or the standards
> have got to change.
> **Jonathan:** Fine. We'll change the standards.
> **William:** I can't change them. If you want to, you
> must go to the very top and convince them.
> Meantime we have to work with the standards as they
> are. So I want you to work out a plan showing how
> you're going to make up the £20,000 in the next
> quarter.
> **Jonathan:** I can't make up the £20,000 in one
> quarter.
> **William:** Can you do it in two?
> **Jonathan:** I can try.

So that's another point. As soon as you've got the facts in focus, move on to the future. Agree a target for future performance, to put things right and make sure the follow-up is established:

> **William:** So you can come back on Friday week?
> **Jonathan:** What for?
> **William:** To show me your plan for cutting £20,000 off the next two quarters' expenditure.
> **Jonathan:** And if I can't?
> **William:** Then it passes out of my hands. I'd have to speak to the Managing Director about it. I'm sorry, but those are the rules.
> **Jonathan:** Friday week? I'll see what I can do.
> **William:** Then we'll look at it again at the end of the month just to make sure it's working properly.

William the Resolute has remembered to fix a date for reviewing the situation, and you, like him, should explain what the procedural consequences will be if there is no improvement by this date. You should also make it clear that you want him to succeed, and that you will be giving him as much help and encouragement as you possibly can during this review time.

So that's it:

1 Establish the gap. Check the facts on standards, check the facts on performance and agree the area of gap.
2 Explore the gap. Ask open questions, listen for the answers and check that it really is a discipline problem and not a grievance or hardship case in disguise.

3 Eliminate the gap. Focus on the facts, look to the future and agree a target, and then fix a review date.

Golden rules

1 The interview is between two people, not a matter for mass communication.
2 Establish and agree the gap between performance and what is required.
3 Discover the reasons for the gap.
4 If you make a special case make sure you tell all concerned.
5 Focus on facts and know yours.
6 Finish with an eye to the future and plan the follow-up.

6 Who's in charge?
The role of the supervisor

Companies, especially large ones, can be a labyrinth of departments, sections and divisions with a multiplicity of staff employed with varying degrees of managerial responsibility from the top executive to the foreman and supervisors who look after the groups who comprise 'the shop floor'. The supervisor level is one whose importance is easily overlooked by the more senior levels of management, and the responsibilities of which can be similarly neglected by the supervisors themselves. Yet no area is

The supervisor level is one
whose importance is easily overlooked

more vital in its demands on 'people management'. This is because the supervisor level, which exists in most medium to large companies even if the title is not used, is the one which **represents the workforce to the management and the management to the workforce**. The chameleon role of the supervisor is by no means easy: it can slip into one or other of the management/ worker 'camps' with disastrous effects. So the management of the supervisors should, automatically, become a key role of the able 'people-oriented' senior manager.

Supervisors, whether of the workers on an assembly belt or of a typing pool, are in charge of a *team*. As such they have responsibilities downwards and upwards – to represent the interests of their team and its members to the more senior level, and to represent the requirements and decisions of senior management to their own staff.

No good manager should divorce himself or herself from the work of their supervisors, partly because within the company it is that vital 'interface' between management and worker and therefore vital to the smooth running of the organisation, and partly because if the supervisor's work is not adequately discharged, essential business can be easily disrupted.

Are these principles easy to follow? Take a girl like Liz who works in the Sales Accounts office of Glendower, Douglas and Scroop. She is an intelligent and likeable woman in her mid-twenties who has been working for the company as a costing clerk. She has experience of computers and has been chosen by her boss, Humphrey Mortimer, to run the office team in the Sales Accounts section. Suddenly she finds herself in charge of half a dozen clerks who, the day before, were her equals. She needs to get them to accept her and the changes she has to make, and also to satisfy Humphrey

Mortimer and his boss, Harry Lancaster, that she can deliver the work. Liz has to do a number of things at once. She has to explain why the new computing system has been chosen and show the others what they will have to do. At the same time she has to advise and encourage each member of staff personally and make sure that they are all pulling their weight. And she has to do a fair share of the work herself, as well as leading the rest of the team. Not an easy situation – especially for someone without any experience of managing other people. Let's see how Humphrey Mortimer prepared Liz for her new position:

Mortimer: Ah, Miss Travers, come in. Shut the door if you would. Sit down. So, are you enjoying computers?

Liz: Very much.

Mortimer: Good. I wanted to have a quiet word with you. You know Mrs Blunt's leaving?

Liz: I knew she was away.

Mortimer: Yes. Her husband's had a stroke, poor man, and she's going to have to spend her time nursing him. The point is, she won't be coming back. And we'd like you to take over.

Liz: What do you mean, take over?

Mortimer: Well, I'd like you to take the post. You know the work. You know the new methods. You're acquainted with everyone in the office, aren't you?

Liz: But I don't have any experience of supervisory work.

Mortimer: Oh, you'll manage. You'll pick it up as you go along. I'm behind you. You don't want to spend the rest of your life number-crunching, do you? I know you think, like I do, that the only way to achieve this reorganisation is to move as swiftly as

we can to on-line computing. I think you could
handle that, couldn't you?

Liz: Yes, I think I could. I'll give it a try.

Mortimer: Well, there's no time like the present, is
there?

Liz: Right.

That was terrible! Liz has received no **proper training** or
backing from the management above her, so she is bound
to make mistakes. It is up to management, in the first
place, to make sure that supervisors like Liz are fully
trained and prepared for the job, and given **adequate
support and advice** while they are doing it. Had Mortimer followed certain elementary guidelines, their conversation would have been totally different. There are five
important points for managers to bear in mind when
they are appointing supervisors:

1 Choose and prepare your supervisors carefully and
   introduce them adequately to their staff.
2 Make clear to them the scope and limits of their
   responsibilities and precisely to whom they are
   responsible.
3 Ensure that they understand and communicate
   their team's objectives.
4 Insist on loyalty both to management and their
   team.
5 Give them continual guidance and support; set
   aside, as a matter of routine, time for properly
   prepared consultation with your supervisors.

But, as we have seen, Humphrey Mortimer followed
none of these principles. He did not even bother to tell
Liz's team of her appointment, or explain to her what
her specific function and responsibilities would be. Inevitably, difficulties soon arise in the office. Pam, who has

been keeping the sales ledger for Mr Mortimer, resents having responsibility taken away from her, and is jealous of Liz's promotion. On the other hand, Kathy, in charge of invoicing, will find she has too much to do. The junior clerks, like Val and Percy, are worried about being made redundant by the new computing system:

Val: Will Mrs Blunt be coming back, do you think?

Liz: No, her husband's in a pretty bad way, I'm afraid.

Percy: Here, do you reckon the firm will take care of her? Or do you think they'll just pass the hat around?

Liz: I don't know.

Pam: What do you mean, Percy?

Percy: Stands to reason, doesn't it, with all this automation. Less staff, it's easy.

Pam: Do you think anybody will lose their job, Liz?

Liz: I don't know.

Kathy: Oh come on. Mortimer must have told you something.

Liz: You know what he's like. Mortimer didn't say anything to me at all.

Val: He wouldn't. Typical.

Liz: Yes, typical. They're all men, aren't they?

Liz is making fatal mistakes here. By not being loyal to the managers above her, she is helping to undermine everyone's confidence in the organisation. At a time when radical new methods are being introduced, this is particularly serious. And now she is going to undermine her staff too by appearing, as she introduces them to the new computer methods, to be altering their responsibilities in an arbitrary way.

Liz: . . . So, Val, you enter the account number and that gives you what is in the ledger at the moment, see? And if you want to change an entry you simply key it in.

Val: Good as the telly, isn't it?

Pam: You've done it wrong now. That's not the proper figure.

Liz: It doesn't matter. I can erase it.

Val: Oh, I'm never going to get the hang of this, you know.

Liz: Of course you will, Val. It's very easy. You OK Pam?

Pam: Yes, I think so. It's like a calculator, really.

Liz: You might think so, but it's more than a calculator. As well as storing what you input, it'll print it out in any order you like.

Pam: And I just take the printouts to Mr Mortimer?

Liz: No, you bring them to me.

Pam: What? I always take the ledger figures straight to Mr Mortimer. And the analyses.

Liz: But I'll have to agree the totals before Mr Mortimer sees them.

Pam: But Mrs Blunt never used to. She always used to leave that to me.

Liz: Well, she wasn't used to working this way. In future I'll set up the schedules and leave you to get the information from the computer. It'll be very easy.

Pam: Yes, I'm sure. What am I supposed to do with the rest of my time? Twiddle my thumbs?

Liz: No, I'd like you to help Val. Give her a hand till she's got the hang of all this.

Pam: And by that time she'll be off having her baby. I'll just be left updating all the records.

Liz: Only temporarily . . .

Terrible again. Pam's confidence has been shaken, long-standing friendships have begun to suffer, rumours and petty jealousies have started to replace effective leadership and communication. Getting nowhere with Liz, Pam feels she has no alternative but to take her problems to Mortimer, further weakening normal chains of command. How will Mortimer respond?

> **Pam:** . . . I don't mind helping out, you ought to know that. It's a question of responsibility. I used to bring my work to you. Now I have to take it to Liz.
>
> **Mortimer:** Yes, well, these are the new routines.
>
> **Pam:** But she gives her mate Kathy responsible work to do. She doesn't give it to me.
>
> **Mortimer:** You'll have to sort that out between you.
>
> **Pam:** What about Val? Are you going to replace her or have I got to do her share of the work?
>
> **Mortimer:** Well, that is entirely Liz's responsibility.
>
> **Pam:** So there *are* going to be redundancies!
>
> **Mortimer:** Ah, well, we certainly oughtn't to need more staff. I'm very busy. Look, give it a chance, Pam, and will you please just try to let things settle down for a few days and help out where you can. I've got a lot on my plate at the moment.

Yes, once again Mortimer is letting Liz down. And also Pam. He should be attempting to reconcile Pam to the new arrangements rather than making things worse by refusing to listen to her properly. And he certainly should have scotched any talk of redundancies. Meanwhile, back in the Sales Accounts office, Liz is adding to the problems:

> **Val:** Liz, about my maternity leave. The firm are supposed to take me back after the baby's born, aren't they?

Liz: I believe so.

Val: Well, can I count on that? I'm not very good on that computer and, well, the thing is I want to come back as soon as possible. Stan's not getting much work now and we're going to have all this expense with the baby and . . .

Liz: Look, Val, it's really not my department. Why don't you go down and talk to Admin?

Val: Will you be keeping my present job open?

Liz: I don't know, Val. Go and talk to Admin. I've got all this work to do for Mr Mortimer.

Liz should not have brushed aside Val's genuine concerns as if they were simply too trivial for her to get involved with. Even if she didn't know the answer to the question, she should have appreciated its importance, shared it, and made it her own business to discover both the legal position and the company's attitude to Val's wish to return after maternity leave. As leader of the team, you must **expect people to come to you for advice**. Indeed you should be worried if they don't. It may not always be convenient or easy; but it is an obligation of your position as well as an act of friendship. You can help simply by being a good listener. People with a genuine problem often have no one with whom they can discuss it, though you will have to learn to differentiate between those with a real need and those who like a moan – which is a need in itself. And remember that the supervisor's role means taking responsibility for the performance of the team and that means involvement with the people concerned both as individuals and as members of that team. It means providing leadership, in the sense of someone prepared to take and share responsibility and also to be the strong

shoulder to lean on when necessary. And as important as anything, it is up to the supervisor's own boss to make sure that such matters are discussed frequently enough to make the supervisor feel supported and the manager informed. Involvement without interference is one of the key roles of the good manager.

Members of your team will come to value your advice if you can offer useful suggestions (such as putting them in touch with welfare services), but not if you make unrealistic promises which are not followed up; and they will respect it more if they know that you always tell them the facts, even when they are unpalatable. Above all, they will appreciate your confidentiality: they may talk about it to the others, but will not expect you to.

It's worth remembering, though, that unsought advice is usually less than welcome, and bad advice is obviously worse than none. So, think carefully before you speak about what is probably very important to the other person.

In this Liz failed Val. In fact, she is failing all the way along the line. Already, as we have seen, Pam is jealous of the 'responsible' work given to Kathy; but has Liz checked to see how Kathy is coping with her invoices and other tasks under the new system? Following Pam's complaints, Mortimer feels impelled to have a word with Liz:

> **Mortimer:** Pam Vernon's been in here complaining about the work you've been giving her.
>
> **Liz:** I only asked her to help Val . . .
>
> **Mortimer:** Pam's an excellent worker but she's a bit touchy. You do realise she was after the supervisor's job herself?
>
> **Liz:** No, I didn't realise.
>
> **Mortimer:** Yes. So please watch how you go with her. I've got enough to do at the moment without people coming in and out of here with silly job squabbles. It is your job to see that everything out there runs smoothly.
>
> **Liz:** What happened, Mr Mortimer, is . . .
>
> **Mortimer:** I don't want to know. I'll leave all that to you.
>
> **Liz:** Did you tell Pam to do what I asked her?
>
> **Mortimer:** Well . . . no . . . I merely suggested she should help out where she could. And incidentally, you do realise there are errors in these customer invoices . . .

So Mortimer has abdicated yet again. He has not demonstrated his support and backing for Liz; he has taken no initiative to discuss the workload problem with her;

he has given her no advice. All he has done is to say, 'Things are bad, it's your job to deal with them,' and pointed out the mistakes on the invoices without, of course, any discussion about how the errors are arising and what could be done to make improvements. It is an angry and worried Liz who rushes back to her department.

> **Liz:** I hear you've been making complaints about me to Mr Mortimer.
> **Pam:** I told him what was going on.
> **Liz:** You'd no right . . .
> **Pam:** I can talk to Mr Mortimer if I want. I always have done.
> **Liz:** Not behind my back. If you have any complaints, you can make them to me. And Kathy! I'd like a word with you. There are several mistakes in these invoice entries. You do check them, don't you?
> **Kathy:** Yes I do. As much as I've time for.
> **Liz:** Then I'd better check them too, in future.

Liz is now desperately trying to assert her authority, instead of listening to, and thinking about, Pam's and Kathy's complaints. She has not delegated properly, so the workload in the office is unfairly spread. It is not surprising that Kathy is making mistakes. The answer is not to attack Kathy for the errors, but to find a way of redistributing the work that is acceptable to everyone. Liz should also attempt to give credit where it is due. Everybody in the office is battling with an unfamiliar system, and it is a trying time for them all. As it is, things in the office are going from bad to worse.

> **Liz:** Mr Mortimer says you're terribly behind with this month's customer accounts.

The colour coding system makes her dizzy . . .

Individual members and their problems are one of your prime responsibilities

Kathy: Are we?
Liz: You know you are, Kathy. I don't know what you've all been doing.
Kathy: Well I can't cope any more. I'm doing half Mrs Blunt's work already.
Liz: It depends how you allocate your other work.
Kathy: It isn't up to me to allocate it. I'm not the supervisor. No one seems to work around here except me.
Liz: We'll have to try a new system.
Kathy: Well, you can try it without me.
Liz: All right, if that's how you feel. Pam, I want you to give me a hand checking these customer statements.
Pam: I can't now.

Liz: Why not?

Pam: Because I'm off. I've done all my work. Anyway, Mr Mortimer said whenever I finished early I could push off. It's no good trying to ask him. He's gone off to a meeting.

Liz: Look, Pam, the office doesn't close for nearly an hour. If we get down to this together we can finish it.

Pam: I've got a date, I'm sorry.

By now it is clear to everyone that the situation is desperate, and Liz gets summoned to Mortimer's office.

Mortimer: This office seems to have become a complete shambles since you took over. I've got a letter here from Kathy. It's a notice of resignation. She's one of our best clerks. And we've been informed that the union have made a complaint that members of our section have been threatened with redundancy. Is that true?

Liz: No, but there were rumours.

Mortimer: It's your job to scotch rumours. The company's given a clear undertaking that there'll be no redundancies as a result of this automation. And why isn't the revenue survey ready? It's wanted for the accountants today.

Liz: I didn't have time.

Mortimer: You should have asked someone like Pam to help you or something.

Liz: She refused.

Mortimer: Refused?

Liz: Yes. She walked out.

Mortimer: Look . . . if she refused, without reason, you should have reported it. You know, there was never any trouble like this when Mrs Blunt was in charge.

Liz: Well, if you feel I'm not up to it, I'd better go back to my old job as a costing clerk.

Liz Travers was unable to lead her team properly, mainly because no one had told her how to do it. As a result, instead of being its centre she found herself an outsider.

A few guidelines will help the supervisor, at any level, to avoid that fate. To start with, make sure that you are **delegating the work sensibly and fairly**, by being careful not to overload willing horses or to withhold responsibility from others. And try to arrange the work so that everyone is contributing to the best of their ability.

A lot of the work will be repetitive and boring – 'number-crunching' in the case of an accounts office like Liz's – but you can make it more attractive and less tedious by conveying your own interest in it to others. 'Giving a lead' is important, and make sure they know *why* your team is having to do it. Although you may not feel it, you are part of the management now, and must be seen to support it. Undermining the company's authority only serves to undermine your own.

The other side of the coin is that your team should know that you will represent them fully and fairly if they have a genuine complaint or reasonable criticism: **loyalty has to go both ways**. Because Liz was not able to discuss her staff's problems effectively with them or with Mortimer, in the end they blew up in her face.

If, unlike her, you face the difficulties as they crop up, you may find yourself involved in a tough decision or a tough interview, but the chances are that your team will be as relieved as you are once the decision is made, provided you have been seen to act with good sense and tact. As you and your team get to know and understand each other better, you'll find that leadership will become a natural part of your job.

In the end, problems like Liz's will rebound not only on her but on her boss. In this case, Mortimer gets, and deserves, a lecture from his own boss, Harry Lancaster. It is clear to Lancaster where the real fault lies.

> **Lancaster:** This girl you chose to take Mrs Blunt's place, Elizabeth Travers, had she any training?
>
> **Mortimer:** Well, no, not so much training as a lot of clerical experience.
>
> **Lancaster:** But had she any computer training?
>
> **Mortimer:** Yes, she'd worked on the computer.
>
> **Lancaster:** And had she any training as a supervisor?
>
> **Mortimer:** . . . I didn't think. It was a matter of time. It was an emergency appointment.
>
> **Lancaster:** I appreciate that, Humphrey, but did you explain to the girl what her duties and responsibilities were going to be?
>
> **Mortimer:** Well, I didn't think there was any need, since she'd worked in the office before.
>
> **Lancaster:** Yes, but not as a supervisor. Did you introduce her to the rest of the staff?
>
> **Mortimer:** She had worked very closely with them before.
>
> **Lancaster:** But not as a supervisor! I mean this appointment is damned important. Don't you realise this girl is at the interface between management and workers. I mean, good God, we're working in a sophisticated industry and we're in a damned tough market.

Lancaster tells Mortimer that it won't do any good to accept Liz's resignation – they can't keep chopping and changing supervisors. The full impact of his failure is brought home to Mortimer and he is a changed man when he next meets Liz:

Mortimer: Mr Lancaster's view is that we should work things out between us. He wants you to stay on in the post.

Liz: But it hasn't worked.

Mortimer: He thinks you've not been given enough support and advice. He wants us to go over the ground together and try to sort it out.

Liz: Right. I'll try.

Mortimer: So we're agreed, then? Don't try to do everything on your own, and come to me if you've got any difficulties. I think we should get the section together and have a chat to them.

Liz: I think I might prefer to do that on my own.

Mortimer: Fine. Then talk to Kathy and Pam alone. Feel free to use my office. But do get the full team together soon, won't you.

Liz: Thank you, I will.

Mortimer: You see, people in our position can't afford to back away from problems. You must listen to what they say, of course, but at the end of the day you are the one with the responsibility. You can come to me if you've got any problems, because I'll back you up.

Liz: Even when I'm wrong?

Mortimer: If I think you're wrong, then I'll talk to you about it afterwards when we're on our own. All right? Have a go.

Later, in the Sales Accounts office.

Liz: I owe you all an apology. It seems I haven't been doing my new job very well.

Percy: Well, it hasn't been easy for any of us.

Liz: What the management have told me is that there'll be no redundancies, no down-grading, so please don't worry about that. Obviously this new system has added its own difficulties. But believe me it really can be a good system if we can just make it work. Obviously there are flaws at the moment. I'm sure you must have some ideas how we can make it better.

Kathy: Well, I was wondering if we should divide up the invoicing differently.

Liz: Divide it up?

Kathy: We could each take a batch of customers and be responsible for them – including the debt-collecting.

Percy: Up to a certain point, when we'd refer them to you. It'd make it much more interesting. We could do our own filing as well.

Liz: Pam, what do you think? It would relieve you of Val's work and give you more time for an analysis.

Pam: So we're staying now, are we Kathy?

Kathy: Oh, I'd stay if we did it like that.

Liz: Pam?

Pam: I never said anything about leaving, did I?

Anyone who leads a team needs to **communicate** with them. Half poor Liz's problems arose because she didn't get all her office staff together at the beginning and talk the job through with them. If she had, she'd have understood better why Pam and Kathy were worried about their workloads and why Val and Percy were worried about redundancies. Naturally, she couldn't know all the answers, but she could have found out from other members of management who did know.

There's little use, of course, in consulting your staff unless you pass on the findings, and any queries they raise, to your boss. It's preferable for him to know what's going on and what people are thinking because you tell him, rather than finding himself faced with unexpected crises. The worst form of company communication is the grapevine! And communication should run sideways, as well as upwards and downwards. It's all too easy, within the confines of your office, to ignore what's happening in other departments and have no idea how your work fits in with the rest. By keeping in touch with your colleagues, the other supervisors, and comparing notes with them, you'll be able to plan your own tasks more intelligently and keep your team more fully aware of the importance and relevance of what they're doing.

Remember, success in leading people is never complete. Things will always go wrong, however hard you try. Nevertheless, the difficulties can be overcome by taking initiatives. Even if you think nobody will let you experiment with an innovation that appears to you to make sense, at least go and ask. If you don't know how to organise a team meeting, go and talk to someone who does. Or better still, study chapter 3! And if you don't have the time for some of the actions you think are important, try to identify some routine tasks which could be delegated in order to give you more scope.

And finally, try to bear in mind one last thought. The job may be difficult and occasionally thankless, but to those who do it well, it can be rewarding and pay dividends. Someone has to be in charge, after all. Why shouldn't it be you?

Golden rules

1 Loyalty must operate upwards and downwards.
2 Be aware of the grapevine and minimise its effect.
3 Respect confidentiality.
4 Leading a team means accepting responsibility for its performance.
5 Remember to give credit where it's due.
6 Teams need to know what is expected of them as a team, and to be told the context in which they are working.
7 Supervising means talking to your team and your boss on a regular basis.

7 This is going to hurt you . . . Giving the bad news

'I'm sorry you haven't got the job in Marketing.'

'I'm afraid we cannot afford to keep you on.'

'You're going to have to work the Christmas shift.'

'Your grades aren't good enough for entry on the scheme.'

Do you recognise them? Telling people they have failed, or been rejected, or their request has been refused, or that after all they are just not good enough for the promotion they were after.

Giving people bad news is part of a manager's job

Giving people bad news is part of a manager's job – a part that most of us dread, that is put off for as long as possible, and even avoided altogether if we think we can get away with it. We don't think about bad news – naturally.

But what happens if we avoid telling someone they cannot have the pay rise they asked for or they haven't got the promotion they sought, until another time?

Well, the knock-on effects of not dealing with bad news will cause far more trouble in the long run. A disappointed employee may well turn into a resentful mutineer – spreading sedition among colleagues. And in real terms what is this going to mean to your organisation and to you as a manager? Failure to co-operate? A downturn in profits?

Bad news is bad news because it's going to injure someone's ego. As a manager there are occasions when you have to give bad news, but you don't have to destroy the employee's pride and confidence in the process.

One important aspect of leadership is caring for individual employees. A leader needs to praise employees' achievements, and to deal with their disappointment professionally and sensitively.

> 'What's the problem? If they can't have their holiday when they want, I just tell them so. Over and done with. No beating about the bush. Problem solved.'

But a bad news interview can have effects that reach far beyond that individual employee's holiday arrangements. A hurt employee will perform badly. Someone who feels humiliation will be suspicious of authority and apathetic towards work. The person is likely to look at the appointments pages in the newspapers.

Bad news interviews which are clumsily handled by managers reduce employees' morale and commitment. What started off as a relatively small problem can lead to a crisis, with far-reaching effects for the organisation.

In fact, conveying the news is not the heart of a bad news interview. **Dealing with the response** is the most important part. And it's the most worrying part for managers.

Yet while the interviewer can't do anything about the bad news itself, careful handling of the interview can alleviate any bitterness the situation may leave behind. And it's the bitterness that leads the disgruntled employee to complain to colleagues about unfairness. This is likely to cause a decline in not just the employee's work but in the work of the rest of the team.

The manager's objective for a bad news interview is not to be loved, but **to deliver the bad news and to gain acceptance of it**. Remember that 'you're not right for this job' is much more hurtful than 'this job is not right for you' and they both mean exactly the same thing. Whatever the situation, the objective remains the same: to convert the employee from someone who is bitter and resentful to someone who may be disappointed but is ready to shake your hand.

Yes, it's hard to break bad news. Especially to people you know well. It is hard when it is your decision you are passing down. It can be even harder when you are asked to convey a decision taken at a more senior level and you personally are unhappy with that decision. But as the manager that is part of the job.

In any circumstance it can be embarrassing and painful. It will certainly be emotional. You will probably be nervous.

As it is part of your job it has to be done. Like other

aspects of leadership there are techniques to learn which can make the task easier. By following them you can limit the damage – to yourself, to your organisation and to your employees.

Prepare the facts

So, let's now look at these techniques. First, inevitably, is preparation. Most managers rush through bad news interviews on the basis that the shorter the interview the less time there is to be embarrassed. Usually the embarrassed interviewers fall into one of the following traps. They are abrupt, peremptory, authoritarian, defensive and sometimes they lose their temper, particularly if the interviewee puts up a fight. It is the classic fight or flight syndrome at work. Most managers see such interviews as a problem and the natural tendency is to get them over quickly with a minimum amount of fuss. This inevitably means they fail to prepare as the preparation in itself causes pain. But that of course is the first mistake.

If you face up to the facts before the interview and prepare before the meeting you are more likely to handle it successfully. You won't be so embarrassed or, in the event of being challenged, so aggressive in your approach. Preparation lowers the confrontation factor.

The first thing to prepare for the interview is the news itself, and the reasons the decision was made. You need to **check all the facts** concerning the case. If you get any of them wrong, your position will be weakened considerably.

A useful tip is to imagine a persistent child asking '*Why?*' to everything you've said/you say.

For example:

> 'I'm afraid you'll have to cover the weekend shift
> yourself.'
> Why?
> 'Because it's your turn.'
> Why?

> 'Because over the last 3 months all the supervisors
> have covered it twice, and you haven't done one
> yet.'
> Why?
> 'Because on 14 January you arranged to swap with
> Sanjit, but you haven't made up the time yet.'
> Etc., etc.

If you are unclear about the reasons behind the decision
your interviewee may go away asking 'Why?' fruitlessly

for weeks afterwards. The chances are the interviewee will come up with more destructive reasons that are really the case.

So Stage One is:

1 Check all the facts concerning the case.
2 Have all the reasons behind the decision to hand.
3 Know why alternative courses were rejected.
4 Anticipate questions and prepare your response to them.
5 Anticipate objections to the news, and have your arguments ready.

Guard the emotions

Once you have gathered together all the information you can, it's time to start thinking about your emotions. You can't say for sure how your interviewee is going to react, but you can start thinking about your emotional responses, bearing the following points in mind:

1 Remember that all the difficult emotions you're really worried about are *yours*.
2 Admit your fears to yourself. In this way you can prevent them from getting in the way at the interview.
3 Assess your employee. How is he/she likely to react? Think of other difficult decisions you have had to share with that person and previous reactions. History has a habit of dictating the future.
4 Work out which are the responses you most dread from your interviewee.
5 Think through how to remain as neutral as possible if the emotional response you dread occurs.

You can't do anything about the news itself, but you can do something about the emotions it arouses. Emotions can be eased, while facts can't. And remember that the more prepared you are, the better able you will be to remain neutral and control your emotions. Your objective is to gain acceptance of the decision by the interviewee. This will be much more difficult to achieve if you let your emotions take over.

So you prepare your facts and **think through your emotions and the likely emotional response of the interviewee**.

Prepare your opening paragraph

The natural next step is to get it over with as quickly as possible; but going in feet first is a recipe for disaster.

There is another very helpful technique before asking the person to a meeting. It is to draft the first paragraph of what you intend to say at the interview. You'll feel much more confident if you have your opening lines already prepared. The kindest way to break bad news is to give that news at the beginning of the meeting. Hence the need to prepare your opening remarks.

1 Prepare a brief lead-in: one or two sentences which explain the relevant background to the decision.
2 Write down how you are going to say the news.
3 Present the decision clearly and unambiguously – even if it sounds a bit blunt.
4 Get to the point quickly and don't flannel.

Prepare the domestic arrangements

So you've prepared the facts, your emotions and your introduction. What else can you do to prepare yourself for the interview? Well, **where**'s the interview going to take place? And **when**? And are you going to have **anyone else present**? Start thinking about logistics.

1 Find a room/area where you won't be overheard: if there is an outburst of emotion you can save the interviewee the additional embarrassment of having it widely known.
2 Allow enough time: it may require at least an hour of talking over and listening.
3 Consider the timing: is it appropriate to deny your production supervisor promotion the day his best-ever production figures came in?
4 Is it useful to bring in an outsider to the interview? Depending on the individual case it may be helpful to have your position backed up by the presence of someone at the highest level. Or – in the worst possible scenario – is there any chance that the interviewee may become violent? You will never be able to achieve your objective if you are worried by the threat of physical violence. Each case must be thought about on an individual basis.
5 Think about how you are going to tell your employee about the interview. Remember that people who are expecting any kind of news will be particularly sensitive. A call over the intercom system asking the staff member to come to the Sales Manager's office is going to cause unnecessary anxiety before you even begin.

Is there any chance that
the interviewee may become violent?

The preparation will take time, but time spent at this stage will save considerable effort later. It may prevent many unnecessary repercussions which are both destructive to your relationship with the employee and could be damaging to the organisation as a whole. If you have done all the possible preparation *before* the interview, you will feel more confident and assured, and you will be well on the way to achieving your objective.

Biting the bullet – giving the bad news

So, your employee knows when the interview is, you've left sufficient time in your diary for the interview, you've arranged a suitable venue and you've prepared all your facts. There's nothing left for you to do now except give the news.

Don't worry. You've written the first paragraph – you have prepared what to say.

Try to **be direct and unambiguous**. People will respect you for being businesslike. Your interviewee will never like the news but will respect your professionalism in the way you conduct the meeting.

Pay attention to your body language. Establish eye contact, otherwise your interviewee is likely to suspect your motives. Tapping your pen on the desk, or fiddling with your hands and your hair is likely to give a signal that you are very nervous. You will look as if you're on the defensive if you sit with your arms folded. At the opposite extreme, standing over the interviewee so they cower in their chair is not going to help the communication process.

But you need to **consider the appropriate level of formality**. No matter how well you know your interviewee the 'drink in the bar after work' approach is always inappropriate. However the 'this is going to hurt me more than it hurts you' approach is also inappropriate. Your pain and embarrassment need to be hidden. If you show them you will weaken your decision and may well antagonise your interviewee.

Assess the interviewee and the situation and behave accordingly. A less assertive person may feel intimidated if you are over-formal.

Remember that during the interview you are representing your organisation and showing concern for the individual. Be clear about your approach and your style of delivery.

DON'TS

1 Don't apologise profusely – it makes you look abject and cringing and does nothing to help the interviewee.

2 Don't use the 'this is going to hurt me more than it hurts you' approach. It's not.

3 Don't say 'I'm very sorry . . .' if you're not. Your face will give away your insincerity.

4 Don't blame the system, your boss, head office – you are your organisation to your employee.

5 Don't say 'The same thing happened to me once, I felt terrible.' The interviewee will not be interested and will resent you.

6 Don't make excuses – a reason is not an excuse.

7 Don't be secretive – you will not be able to gain acceptance of the decision if you answer questions with 'I'm not in a position to tell you why.'

8 Don't 'blind them with science': complicated language or over-elaborate explanations look like flannel.

9 Don't negotiate. The decision is the decision. You should not be holding the interview unless you have reached the end of the line in terms of options.

10 Don't interrupt.

11 Don't point your finger, shake your head or frown.

DO'S

1 Be clear and firm. Adopt a businesslike attitude.

2 Deliver the news.

3 Retain a degree of formality.

4 Use a brief lead-in to soften the blow.

5 Establish and maintain eye contact.

6 Control your embarrassment and emotions.

7 Be honest – reasons must be given in as full and open a manner as the occasion allows.
8 Use appropriate body language.

Listening to the response – dealing with the individual

Every individual responds differently to bad news. It is vital at this stage to think on your feet, to be flexible in your behaviour.

This of course is where your preparation will be helpful. It is likely to give you clues as to how the person will behave.

For example, a promotion turndown to one person may generate the response, 'Well, it was worth a try. I needed interview practice anyway'. Another candidate may be devastated because he/she may have more than a bruised ego on the line. Perhaps they have financial problems, or they don't get on with their current colleagues, or just can't do the same job any longer.

There are no reference books you can consult for useful phrases to use in various circumstances.

Your first task is to **listen actively** to the interviewee's response. You need to find out how they feel so that you can understand how they feel. Your interviewee will not think he/she has been given a fair hearing if you fail to listen to their point of view or demonstrate that you are taking their reaction seriously.

Active listening involves:

1 Making listening noises such as 'I see', 'Right', etc.
2 Matching body language to the words being said. If you are saying 'I think this is important too', but

are looking out of the window, you will not be very convincing.

3 Concentrating on the matter in hand. Doodling or reading other documents at the same time as appearing to be listening will indicate that you are uncaring, unfeeling and not listening properly.

After all, you are asking your interviewee to accept a decision which goes against him or her. Gaining that acceptance will be achieved only if what you say is well reasoned, how you say it is well delivered and your subsequent behaviour implies that you take the matter and the person's response seriously.

Reaction to the response –
handling the interviewee's emotions

There are three basic ways people respond to bad news:

1 They get emotional, e.g. cry or get hysterical
2 They clam up
3 They argue

All three require different responses from you the interviewer. But in all three cases you need to **remain emotionally neutral.**

Let's deal with each possible response in turn. This is where your preparation also comes in useful.

PEOPLE WHO
GET EMOTIONAL

For many managers emotional subjects are the ones they dread most. Most managers dread dealing with the employee who bursts into tears. On bad news occasions tears are a fairly typical response. A chauvinistic response is to believe that all females cry when given bad news. But, if the truth be known, male employees cry as well and many female managers find that just as embarrassing as their male counterparts.

You may feel uncomfortable if confronted by a weeping employee but many psychologists would say that tears are the first stage in the healing process.

So, how can you best respond to an emotional employee? **Let them work through their tears or anger** and do not cut them off because you can't cope with this response.

Don't ignore them, or look out of the window, but give them time to work their feelings through. Difficult as it may seem, you just need to sit and wait.

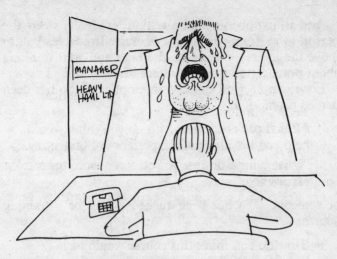

Let them work through their tears

Don't attempt to shout them down. Giving vent to feelings of anger, grief or disappointment often makes the person feel better. Such emotional displays usually come to a halt of their own accord.

Don't take the person's abuse or anger as directed against you personally. You need to divorce your leadership role from your personal feelings. You may be temporarily the target of the person's anger – but not the object of it. Let any abuse wash over you.

Once the emotion has started to ebb, **start asking the employee open questions**. It shows you're listening and that you are taking their response seriously. Very often you find that the real cause of the person's concern may be something different. Perhaps they have requested a transfer to another department because they don't get on with their colleagues, or they feel unable to cope with new technology, or resent a change in shift patterns.

And asking open-ended questions gradually steers the person away from the source of hurt. It enables you to move the interview towards the facts and start thinking about practical solutions or alternatives.

For example, you can ask an employee who has been denied promotion:

> 'Which projects coming up do you think would help you broaden your experience of budgeting?'

> 'What can we do to give you some more practical experience?'

or someone who has been turned down for a training course:

> 'How do you think this course would have benefited you?'

> 'Where do you see yourself going after finishing your training?'

And to someone who has been made redundant:

> 'How do you feel about retraining courses at the local college?'

> 'When do you think you'll be ready to discuss the alternatives with the counsellor?'

So, if the person gets emotional, ride out the storm by:

1 Letting them work through their tears or anger.
2 Listening and continually showing you understand.
3 Allowing any abuse to wash over you.
4 Starting to ask open questions, once the storm has begun to recede.
5 Not interrupting or getting emotional yourself.

PEOPLE WHO CLAM UP

Some people will respond to even the worst news by total silence. This may relieve the manager who may have been expecting some kind of outburst. But you mustn't assume that people aren't upset just because they clam up. Remember that you can't help people to accept unwelcome news until you've listened to their response to it.

If you don't get any response from a silent employee, they may later collapse with grief, or give vent to anger or express their disappointment elsewhere. You cannot assume that you have gained your interviewee's acceptance of the news because they haven't reacted to it. Silence *is* a reaction. Deal with it like any other response. How? First of all find out what the person is feeling. Ask questions, and allow time to respond. Again, sit it out and wait.

It is no use just asking closed questions based on assumptions of how that person is feeling.

'Do you need a holiday?'

'Any problems at home?'

'Haven't you been feeling well?'

This type of questioning will not elicit any response from a silent employee. You need to really probe – ask open questions. And allow time for a response. Don't put words into his/her mouth.

There is a prevalent feeling in such situations that you have to keep up the conversation all the time. But this will only help cover your unease and embarrassment. It will not help the interviewee at all. He or she needs time to think.

Don't put words into his/her mouth

Silence can be an important tool in getting people to talk about their feelings; use it, don't try to break the silence because the silence makes you feel uncomfortable. If the interviewee does clam up, **probe for a response** by:

1 Asking open-ended questions.
2 Giving the person time to respond, without being hurried.
3 Not interrupting or putting words into his/her mouth.
4 Encouraging the person to talk.
5 Showing you have time to listen and want to understand.

PEOPLE WHO ARGUE

Most managers dread this response, the employee who argues. This is the employee who will try to change the manager's mind or attempt to call his bluff. They may attempt to negotiate, or offer alternatives to the decision.

This is where you will benefit from the time spent preparing all the facts. Make it clear that the decision is final, be able to explain the reasons behind the decision and why alternative courses of action have been rejected. It is a mistake, in the face of argument, to attempt to come up with other reasons for the decision on the spur of the moment. What you say won't have been prepared – and it will look to the employee like flannel.

Concentrate on the facts – re-stating them calmly and firmly if necessary. If the person takes a stand, search for the reasons behind the stand, rather than attacking the stand itself.

Do not make the mistake of pulling rank, or hiding behind your authority. 'I'm the boss, what I say goes'. You need to gain acceptance of the decision without over-exerting your more senior status. The management of the situation needs to be underplayed and barely noticeable.

Appropriate body language is essential. Crossed arms will look defensive and only encourage the person to continue attacking. But reacting to anger by aggressive gestures such as finger-pointing, or by frowning or shaking your head will come across as responding to anger with anger. It will do nothing to control or calm down the employee. If the interviewee is aggressive, lower your voice. It helps to make 'lowering' gestures with your hands.

Above all **stay neutral and dispassionate**.
So if the employee argues, stand your ground by:

1 Giving the news coolly and firmly.
2 Re-stating the decision. Do not come up with other reasons on the spur of the moment.
3 Underplaying the situation: not over-exerting your authority.
4 Responding to anger with calm gestures.
5 Staying cool; remaining neutral and dispassionate.

You are undoubtedly going to have to think on your feet during the interview, dealing with each response as it arises. But as general principles, remember:

1 If the person gets emotional, ride the storm.
2 If they clam up, probe.
3 If they argue, stand your ground.

How can I help? – limiting the damage

There comes a point when you need to start steering people away from their present emotions towards the future.

Use your judgement to analyse when that point is, but it's when you think all the emotions have come out and you've begun to hear it all the second time round. And what do you do then? Start thinking about how your interviewee is likely to feel when they've calmed down. And work out ways you can help them. You need to limit the damage as far as possible. Remember they have:

1 Just received some unwelcome news
2 Reacted to the news, exposing strong emotions and feelings

Egos have been bruised. The interviewee will be feeling disappointed and lacking in self-esteem. You need first of all to **put the decision in perspective**.

The person needs to be reassured that because they have been made redundant, it doesn't mean they are an abject failure. Or because they didn't get promotion this time they have no future.

Feeling a failure is the natural response to bad news. Self-esteem shrinks – often out of all proportion to what's actually happened.

Employees become blind to their own strengths. As a manager, remind them of their abilities, and where possible offer constructive advice for the future. If at all appropriate, stress the positive side of their achievements to date and let the person know they have your support.

Next, start thinking about **letting other people know the news**. This may not always be necessary, but most employees like to have this problem resolved for them. Talk to the employee, ask for his or her views on how the news should be broken, where, when, and to whom. Offer suggestions and alternatives – but make it clear that their views will be respected. So, if the news has to be made public, discuss with your employee how it is going to be announced.

A decision has to be made quickly. The employee will otherwise worry about whether or not colleagues know the news, and they will not be able to return to any sense of normality.

Thirdly, start talking to the person about their **future opportunities**. They are bound to feel apprehensive about it, but you may be able to offer them compensations. Help the employee to work out why they didn't get the promotion they were after. Are there any additional areas of responsibility they could take on? Can you suggest any retraining courses for your redundant employee? Or is this an opportunity for them to set up on their own? But if there aren't any compensations, don't fabricate them. Make an effort to be more supportive than usual in the short term.

And finally, put the interview out of your head afterwards. The employee may feel acutely embarrassed for crying or for shouting at you. Make it clear you won't use any emotional outburst against them, carry on as if nothing had happened.

Remember, then, that a bad news interview should end on some form of discussion about what happens now, next steps, and the future. After delivering the news and listening to the response, you need to limit the damage by:

1 Putting the news in perspective.
2 Discussing how it will be announced.
3 Talking about future opportunities.

Golden rules

1 Giving the news is not difficult; dealing with the response can be.
2 The job is to gain acceptance of an unwelcome decision.
3 Anticipate the response and prepare by imagining the response 'Why?' after every point you intend to raise.
4 Guard your own emotions.
5 Write down your opening remarks as a paragraph.
6 Get to the point quickly.
7 Listen actively and don't argue.
8 Don't fill silence, wait until there is a response.
9 Do not parade authority but stick to your ground.
10 If possible, find a positive but genuine gesture regarding the future.
11 If a public announcement is necessary, make sure that the person has had his or her say on what, how and when.

Video Arts

World Leaders in Video Training Programmes

For information about hiring or buying
Video Arts training films please contact:

Video Arts Ltd
Dumbarton House
68 Oxford Street
London WIN 9LA

Tel: 071 637 7288
Fax: 071 580 8103